THE LIBRARY—CENTERED

APPROACH TO LEARNING

THE LIBRARY–CENTERED
APPROACH TO LEARNING

by

Sister Marie Schuster

AN ETC PUBLICATION

TABLE OF CONTENTS

Introduction vi

One   The Nature of the Learner and of the
Learning Process 1

Two   The Learning Facilitator 12

Three   The Learning Environment 22

Four   A Library-College Concept 32

Five   A Library-Centered Approach to Learning
in the Junior High School 42

Six   Learning in the Primary School Library 54

Seven   Implementing Library-Centered Learning 64

Eight   The Wholeness of a Library-Centered
Approach to Learning 76

Nine   Reading: An Experience of Wholeness 86

Ten   Writing: A Personal Response 92

Eleven   Learning through Insight. 96

Twelve   The Transcendental Dimension of the
Learner 100

Bibliography 105

Index. 110

C P

Library of Congress Cataloging in Publication Data

Schuster, Marie,   1936 —

   The library-centered approach to learning.

      Bibliography: p.
      Includes index.

      1. Libraries and education. 2. Libraries and schools.
   3. Education — Aims and objectives. I. Title

   Z718.S34   021'.24   76-54328

   ISBN 0-88280-047-7

Copyright · © 1977 by   ETC PUBLICATIONS
                        Palm Springs
                        California 92262

INTRODUCTION

Education which is real is necessarily learner-centered. It is based on learner needs and nourished learner growth. It assists the learner in the process of becoming a whole and fully—functioning person.

Such education is provided best through a library-centered approach to learning. The library-centered approach realizes learning as a creative process. In contrast with educational methods which are concerned with the end-product, with a well-trained, efficient, even knowledgeable alumni, the library-centered approach is concerned with learning as a life-long process of growth.

This discussion of the nature of the learner and of the learning process, of the learning facilitator and environment, and of library-centered learning, attempts to present a vision of education which is whole and which creates wholeness within and among all learners.

THE LIBRARY–CENTERED

APPROACH TO LEARNING

Chapter One
The Nature of the Learner
and of the
Learning Process

Libraries exist for the sake of learners. Therefore, an understanding of the nature of the learner and of the learning process is necessary to a consideration of the function of the library. This discussion of wholeness as related to learning in the library begins, therefore, with a description of the learner and of the learning process.

The nature of living things demands that they grow. This law holds true for all of life, from the simple ameba to the most complex creature, man. Growth occurs not only during the early years of life; it is a process which is synonymous with life itself. It is the process through which life comes to maturity; therefore, growth is a life-long process. To live is to grow, and to grow is to change.

As life grows to maturity, it undergoes many changes; and as human life matures, it experiences the greatest change possible. The greatest change which can occur within the human person is that he increase in consciousness. This growth in consciousness means that the person becomes ever more aware of himself, other people, and the stuff of the universe. This awareness or consciousness differentiates the human person from all other forms of life, and as the person continually increases in consciousness, he more fully becomes all that he can become.

Changing the level of consciousness may be understood as the process of learning. This process changes the learner from within himself. It changes his feelings, ideas, decisions, and actions. It gives him new awarenesses, new insights. The process of learning brings to the learner greater knowledge and fuller understandings. Because this learning act increase the level of consciousness, it is a growth process, and because it is a growth process, it effects permanent changes within the learner.

The increase in level of consciousness happens through the learner's response to life. A response may be any form of conscious attention given some one or some thing. This response may mean that the learner looks upon an object, listens to a sound, or reflects upon an idea. The response may include the use of any of the senses or powers of the mind. Whatever his response, through it the learner increases the depth of his awareness.

The learner's response to life is a form of communication. In the act of responding to another person, an idea, a thing, or whatever, the learner and that to which he responds realize a mutual sharing between them. This mutual sharing means that the learner becomes a part of that to which he has responded, while the latter receives a participation in the life of the learner. The mutual interaction is a form of communication which establishes a communion, a oneness, between the learner and his world.

The communication thus realized releases creative energies. These creative energies are inherent powers which permeate the world of people and of stuff. When released or called forth or permitted to become through human communication, they produce a unique person or other work of creation. Therefore, learning, which begins with the learner's response to life's demand to grow, results finally in an act of creation.

The learner is intrinsically free, and his response to life is by nature an act of freedom. This freedom consists essentially in the innate power to choose one's response. Regardless of the situation in which the learner finds himself, he is always free to choose his response to it. He is free to participate in his world, thereby becoming more aware of it. As he exercises his power of free choice the learner shares in the creative powers of the universe and learns to become master of his world.

However, the learner is also free to refuse his responsibility for growth. He may refuse the opportunity to change his level of consciousness. He is free to take for granted or ignore the stuff of the universe, thereby remaining in blindness. He is free to choose a response which thwarts his growth. He may even feel that a situation controls him because it defines his choices. However, he cannot lose or be deprived of the freedom to choose his response. Such freedom lasts as long as life.

In an essay on the education of man, Heinrich Pestalozzi expresses the idea that the purpose of education is to help man realize this innate freedom. "The higher purpose of education is to prepare the individual to make free and self-reliant use of all the faculties with which the Creator has endowed him, and so to direct these faculties that they may perfect all human life; each individual, in his proper place, should be able to act as the instrument of the omnipotent, all-knowing Power that has called him into being."[1]

Because the learner always enjoys the ability to be aware and the freedom to choose his responses to these awarenesses, he has within him the means for life-long learning. The realization that learning is a life-long process results in a sense of security, an independence, and a freedom from fear. The life-long learner acquires these traits as he comes to know that the awful powers which he possesses can continually be released and thereby create a new person.

The learner knows that the power of self-creation with its inherent freedom is a permanent source of inner strength for him as he encounters new experiences. Therefore, his approach to the new, as to all of life, is without fear, for fear is inevitable only as long as the mind is seeking security. The mind that is free no longer searches for security for it understands that the only real security exists in the free use of one's powers.

As the learner creates himself, he becomes increasingly aware of his responsibility for who he is. Because he knows that he is SOME ONE, distinct from all other persons, and that he is responsible for creating himself, he develops a security based primarily on his own inner resources, rather than on the acceptance and approval of others. As Carl Rogers has said, "The only man who is educated is the man who has learned how to learn; the man who has learned how to adapt and change; the man who has realized that no knowledge is secure, that only the process of seeking knowledge gives a basis for security. Changingness, a reliance on the process rather than upon static knowledge, is the only thing that makes any sense as a goal for education in the modern world."[2]

In the process of learning how to learn, of learning how to adapt and change, the learner becomes even more aware of his powers, of himself as a functioning being. Therefore, he also realizes an independence from others. This independence consists not in a negative detachment from others, but rather in a positive realization that his distinction contributes to the unity of all, that only his uniqueness can complement the lives of others. Therefore, the learner follows nature's demand that he become a unique self.

Since learning is to be as continual as life itself, nature has fitted the learner with those qualities which learning requires. The primary requirement for learning to happen is that the learner be open to experience. The openness includes a willingness to be changed by these encounters with life.

The poet Tennyson expresses the attitude and approach of one who would "drink life to the lees." In his poem, "Ulysses," he tells of the desire to encounter and to be changed by life's experiences. He says that all experiences of life become a part of one and that many more opportunities for growth lie ahead. He expresses a thirst for a life full of challenge, of knowledge, of new things. Tennyson writes:

"I am a part of all that I have met;
Yet all experience is an arch wherethro'
Gleams that untravell'd world whose margin fades
For ever and for ever when I move.
How dull it is to pause, to make an end,
To rust unburnishe'd not to shine in use!
As tho' to breathe were life! Life piled on life
Were all too little, and of one to me
Little remains; but every hour is saved
From that eternal silence, something more,
A bringer of new things; and vile it were
For some three suns to store and hoard myself,
And this gray spirit yearning in desire
To follow knowledge like a sinking star,
Beyond the utmost bound of human tbought."[3]

The learner who is open to experience acknowledges his innate need and desire for understandings. He is aware of his yearning to learn and thereby to be changed. He acknowledges his need to be reoriented to his world. That is, he needs to become continually aware of his temporal, spacial, and personal relationships. He recognizes his need to see himself and his world in relationship in order to have an integrated world view.

When relationships are integrated, the learner is able to order his values. He is able to see one value in relationship to another value and to the whole. Because he is aware of the wholeness of his life, he is able to discriminate intelligently among relative values and to make choices. The learner who is open to experience knows that his learning needs can be fulfilled throughout his life.

The learner fulfills his needs through the learning process which is personal. The personal nature of this process is indicated in the words of Everett Dean Martin who writes of learning as an adventure in truth-seeking and as a venture in spiritual freedom. Such processes can only be personal. They are of the spirit of learning, and this spirit arises from within the learner, being as unique as himself. A common erroneous ". . . presupposition is that the important factor in education is the question what is to be taught, rather than the spirit of learning itself. Education is conceived of as knowledge acquired. Attention is fixed not on the learning process through which an individual becomes reoriented to his world, but upon the end result, something fixed and done, a certain amount of information stored up. Is this what we mean by learning? Is it receiving and memorizing a given something either cultural or practical? Or is it an adventure in any kind of truth seeking which changes the quality of one's future experience and enables one to behave not merely efficiently but wisely, with a broad view and a sympathetic understanding of the many ways in which men have striven to create meaning and value out of the possibilities of human life? If this last is correct, the real question is not what shall be learned but how and why and to what end. Is learning a venture in spiritual freedom that is humanism, or is it a routine process of animal training?"[4]

Martin continues by saying of education that "It is a spiritual awakening; and if this awakening does not come, a person is not being educated however much he knows."[5] This spiritual awakening may be understood as an increase of consciousness, which, in turn, has been described as learning.

Learning is change, but no one can change another; one can only allow himself to be changed from within. The learner changes only as he responds to life. His response releases his creative energies and frees his innate powers. The way in which a learner meets and responds to a new experience has been described by John Holt, who refers to such a learner as an intelligent person. "The intelligent person, young or old, meeting a new situation or problem, opens himself up to it; he tries to take in with mind and senses everything he can about it; he thinks about IT, instead of about himself or what it might cause to happen to him; he grapples with it boldly, imaginatively, resourcefully, and if not confidently at least hopefully; if he fails to master it, he looks without shame or fear at his mistakes and learns what he can from them."[6] Through this process the learner satisfies his personal learning needs.

When the learner is open to experience, he exercises what may be the most intense of all activities; namely, that of listening. He listens in order to learn. To listen is to let one's attention be concentrated on a message, but the message cannot be separated from the messenger. Therefore, to receive within oneself the messages of the universe, to reflect on these and make them one's own, effects an integration of the learner with other persons and with his world. Thereby listening becomes a means of integration.

] 5 [

The learner listens to himself, thus creating self-knowledge. To listen to himself is to be aware of his feelings, prejudices, opinions, ideas. It is to be aware of how and why, when, to whom, and to what he responds. To listen to himself is to give attention to his dreams and intuitions, to his words, both spoken and unspoken, to his insights and blindness, and to all the promptings of the heart. The learner who listens to himself in all of these ways arrives at a marked degree of self-knowledge, which is necessary for the learning process to mature.

The learner listens also to other people, thereby creating human understanding. To listen to others requires that he shut off the flow of thoughts within himself, so that not distracted by what he plans to say next, he can be open, receptive, and give his full attention to the other person. This attitude is quite different from that of the person who listens, not to the words spoken by the other, but only for a chance to begin talking himself. As he listens to others, the learner becomes aware of the feelings and ideas of others. He broadens his world-view by making his own these new awarenesses gleaned through listening, and he creates human understanding as he takes into himself the words of the other.

Finally, the learner listens to the entire world of experiences which provide further opportunity for his growth. He is attentive to the happenings of daily life, to the evolving processes of that life. He is aware of interrelationships among people as well as of structures of the cosmos. He is open to everything because he is still within himself. Such openness, receptivity, listening, is a requisite for creation. "When the mind is utterly still without being forced or trained into quiescence, when it is silent because the self is inactive, then there is creation."[7]

Listening is a personal activity which produces a permanent change in the listener. It influences his thoughts, actions and emotions. It makes him aware of his own poverty. The listener is aware of how large life is and how small he is; therefore, he sees his need to grow toward greater fulfillment. Acknowledging his own emptiness, he begins to understand his need to be fulfilled through union with his fellowmen and his world. The listener realizes this union through a growing knowledge and understanding of himself and of his world.

One who is open to experience, who has learned to listen, and listens in order to learn, develops within himself an attitude of humility, that is, an honest insight into who he is and who he can become. The learner who is humble has the conviction that he can learn, that he can change. Therefore, he values himself. He has put his world in order and has found a place for himself in it. He is at peace with himself because he has acquired interior order and harmony.

Openness to experience and the ability to listen are the prerequisites for the evolution of the learner's creative ability. This creative ability includes the power to create oneself through one's responses to life and the power to contribute toward the creation of the world. The act of creation brings truth into the world. But truth is brought into being only by the learner who possesses integrity. Therefore, the learner who would create himself and his world is characterized as integral. The person who is integral possesses himself as a whole and complete being. He acknowledges both his abilities and his limitations. He knows who he is and lives that knowledge. He is capable of creation because it is an extension of his own true self. The learner who is not integral cannot create fuller life; he can only cause perversions.

The truth thus brought into being is revealed through the learner's self-expression. The learner reveals his unique self as he expresses the new reality which he has become through the learning process. This self-expression, in order to be authentic, has its basis in self-knowledge, since without self-knowledge, self-expression becomes merely a form of self-assertion. Such self-assertion cannot be true communication because it springs not from the real self which one is but from a lack of real being, characterized by insecurity. The insecure self asserts itself through aggressive and ambitious behavior. The secure self expresses his authentic self, since he who creates himself through the learning process values himself and enjoys the freedom and the courage to express himself honestly. For such a learner there is complete accord between who he is and who he reveals himself to be.

On the other hand, the learning process does not merely provide the opportunity to indulge in gratifying self-expression. Rather it awakens within the individual the capacity to be self-aware since such self-awareness is a requisite for authentic communication of the self. The learner who is self-aware learns naturally. John Holt writes that: ". . . a child who is learning naturally, following his curiosity where it leads him, adding to his mental model of reality whatever he needs and can find a place for, and rejecting without fear or guilt what he does not need, is growing — in knowledge, in the love of learning, and in the ability to learn . . . All his life he will go on learning. Every experience will make his mental model of reality more complete and more true to life, and thus make him more able to deal realistically, imaginatively, and constructively with whatever new experience life throws his way."8

Thus far the learner has been described as one who freely responds to nature's demand to grow and who therefore becomes ever more conscious of himself and his world. He communicates with his world, thereby releasing the creative energies of the universe. He acknowledges his need to be open to experience, to listen, and to become a life-long learner who enjoys security and independence. Such a learner brings truth into being through his power of authentic self-expression. All of these characteristics are natural to the human person. Everyone is a learner according to these terms.

In addition, the learning process can bring the learner to a marked degree of wholeness. An individual who realizes this wholeness may be considered a fully-functioning person. The wholeness of the fully-functioning person includes several characteristics.

The individual who is fully-functioning possesses a positive view of self. This positive attitude enables him to accept himself as a dynamic, ever-changing, person-in-process whose nature predisposes him to growth. Because of his positive attitude he trusts his own human nature and his own experiencing. Because he trusts himself, he sees the value of his mistakes. He accepts his mistakes, not as evidences of failure, but as further opportunities for insights. This acceptance and trust of self enables the learner to experience himself as a responsible person in process of fulfillment.

Because of his positive self-concept, the fully-functioning person is able to value others. His own self-respect and sense of dignity grow out of his increasing self-understanding, which in turn forms the basis for his respect for the rights and differences of others. He not only trusts his own nature, but he recognizes the trustworthiness of all human nature.

The fully-functioning person possesses a knowledge of his own identity and experiences learning as a process of ever increasing individuation. The individuation process includes a coming to terms with the inherent germ of wholeness and circumstances of life as well as with the unconscious force actively at work deep within each learner. As he realizes his uniqueness, his distinction from others, and his own identity, he simultaneously realizes his unity and his identification with others. He sees his stake in others. He sees that greater fulfillment of his own being effects greater unity among persons. Therefore, in the learning process through which he achieves his independence, he also achieves an interdependence with others.

The fully-functioning person lives his life as a process. He sees himself as part of a world in movement. He accepts each moment of life as a continuation of a series of new awarenesses of further evolution of his consciousness. For him there are no new beginnings rather each moment contains the sum of all past experiences combined with the yet untried potential of the present. For one who lives his life as a process, each moment is a richer, fuller, evolution of all that life has ever been and is a fresh opportunity for creative energies to be released and directed. Therefore, the fully-functioning person is intrinsically creative.

The creative person, who is also the fully-functioning person, sees the world-in-process as open-ended, without limits; and he sees himself as a participant in it. He knows his world as an extension of himself, since he realizes his interrelatedness with it. This idea of interrelatedness may be expressed in these words of Walt Whitman:

"There was a child went forth every day,
and the first object he look'd upon,
that object he became,
And that object became part of him for the
day or a certain part of the day,
Or for many years or stretching cycles of years . . ."9

The learner who attains the wholeness of the fully-functioning person listens to, receives into his being, and is fulfilled by all things which are meaningful for him; and things are meaningful insofar as they relate to his own needs and discoveries. Their meaning is not discovered once for all, but is rediscovered with each new experience.

These experiences and the learner's response to them are not isolated elements in an individual's life, but are an extension of his whole bring. In the life of the fully-functioning person, who is a whole person, all of the experiences and responses are identifiable with his entire being. Such an individual is not composed of various elements, but is an integral whole. Every aspect of his life situation interrelates with every other and with the whole. The way in which he responds to one experience affects the way in which he responds to subsequent experiences. That is, way leads on to way. Gradually, the learner's responses form a pattern, and the entire pattern of his life occurs within a structure. The structure provides the wholeness within which the learner experiences life.

Within this structure every response remains a free choice. Every response requires a decision which may appear to limit the growth process, but which in fact opens it to ever more possibilities. The poetic words of Robert Frost describe the individual exercising his power of responsible choice and the consequence:

"Two roads diverged in a yellow wood,
And sorry I could not travel both
And be one traveler, long I stood
And looked down one as far as I could

. . .

Then took the other,. . .
Oh, I kept the first for another day!
Yet knowing how way leads on to way,
I doubted if I should ever come back.

. . .

Two roads diverged in a wood, and I ——
I took the one less traveled by,
And that has made all the difference."[10]

In exercising his responsible freedom, the poet, as well as every learner, acts according to his nature. Because by nature the learner is free, the challenge of those involved in the learning process is to provide opportunities for the exercise of freedom. Such freedom includes that of learning how to learn, to change, to grow in consciousness, to become mature.

This learning process occurs in environments which respect the learner's nature and thereby meet the learner's needs. Subsequent chapters will attempt to show that a library-centered learning environment provides the perfect opportunity for satisfying the learner's needs, while the most important element of the learning environment, that is, the learning facilitator, will be discussed next.

1 Heinrich Pestalozzi, *The Education of Man: Aphorisms,* p. 31

2 Carl R. Rogers, *Freedom to Learn,* p. 104.

3 Alfred Lord Tennyson, *The Poems and Plays of Alfred Lord Tennyson,* p. 166-168.

4 Everett Dean Martin, *The Meaning of a Liberal Education,* p. 27.

5 Ibid., p. 43.

6 John Holt, *How Children Fail,* p. 165.

7 Jiddu Krishnamurti, *Education and the Significance of Life,* p. 125.

8 Holt, p. 178.

9 Walt Whitman, *Leaves of Grass,* p. 288.

10 Robert Frost, *The Poems of Robert Frost,* p. 117

Chapter Two
The Learning Facilitator

Within the learning environment the learner may be assisted by a facilitator. A facilitator is one who nurtures the process of growth within the learner. He does this by providing the learner with opportunities to communicate with his world.

The facilitator provides opportunities for communication when he brings together the learner and the tools of learning. In doing this he can stimulate the learner's desire to learn. He can describe, explain, show and tell; but he cannot give knowledge or understandings or wisdom. For these the learner must change himself from within. The facilitator cannot teach the learner anything; he can only provide the opportunity to learn.

In his book, THE PROPHET, Kahlil Gibran speaks of teaching, indicating its limitations and its possibilities. The teacher is limited because he cannot give his knowledge or understandings or wisdom to the learner; however, he has the possibility of leading the learner to the threshold of his own mind. The teacher cannot impose information or ideas upon the student, but he can be for the student an exemplar of receptivity to new understandings.

"Then said a teacher, speak to us of teaching. And he said: No man can reveal to you aught but that which already lies half asleep in the dawning of your knowledge.

The teacher who walks in the shadow of the temple, among his followers, gives not of his wisdom but rather of his faith and his lovingness.

If he is indeed wise he does not bid you enter the house of his wisdom, but rather leads you to the threshold of your own mind.

The astronomer may speak to you of his understanding of space, but he cannot give you his understanding.

The musician may sing to you of the rhythm which is in all space, but he cannot give you the ear which arrests the rhythm nor the voice that echoes it.

And he who is versed in the science of numbers can tell of

the regions of weight and measure, but he cannot conduct you thither.

For the vision of one man lends not its wings to another man.

And even as each one of you stands alone in God's knowledge, so must each one of you be alone in his knowledge of God and in understanding of the earth."[1]

The facilitator may perform the functions often attributed to a teacher or librarian; however, it is as a person, rather than as a functionary, that the impact of the facilitator is felt. It is in the person of the facilitator, rather than in the curriculum or organization of the school, that all elements of learning are harmonized: skills, knowledge, understandings, values, persons, and relationships between persons. The personal relationship between facilitator and learner determines whether or not significant learnings will occur. Neither technology nor methods derived from the most careful research can take the place of the heart and soul of the teacher.

The learner responds to the facilitator for who he is; therefore, he must be SOME ONE; he must be himself. Studies on the teacher's use of the self as an instrument in helping others learn show statistically significant differences between groups of effective and ineffective teachers. Part of this difference lies in the way teachers view themselves, in their self-concept. "Effective teachers tend to view themselves as identified with others, capable of solving problems, dependable, and more worthy than unworthy. In simple terms, they have developed feelings of adequacy which enable them to take a courageous approach to the tasks of life. They are not hampered by insecurities, doubts, and fears which neurologically short-circuit their capacity to be fully functioning persons and professionals. They possess positive attitudes toward themselves and their potential. They have not been emotionally crippled by society, the culture, or even the classroom which emphasizes faults, liabilities, and mistakes."[2]

Because the effective teacher possesses a positive self-concept, he tends to see others also in a positive way; that is, as friendly, well-intentioned, and capable of dealing successfully with their problems. The positive attitude toward others enables the facilitator to accept the learner as a whole person, having feelings, values and attitudes, as well as opinions and ideas. Therefore, the facilitator touches both the affective and the cognitive domain. Studies show that "Effective teachers are concerned with: (1) internal rather than external frames of reference, (2) people rather than things, and (3) perceptual meanings rather than facts. They are sensitive to the feelings of students and perceive them as persons, not as objects to be taught, studied, or analyzed. They are more concerned with persons and their reactions than with the material they are presenting."[3] Only a facilitator with a positive self-concept and with positive attitudes toward others can be a fully-functioning person able to meet the current challenges in education.

The facilitator who is fully-functioning incorporates himself deeply into his every attitude and act. Because his behavior accords with his being, he can be described as possessing specific characteristics. Some of the characteristics of teachers who may be considered outstanding are "Superior intellectual abilities, above-average school achievement, good emotional adjustment, attitudes favorable to pupils, enjoyment of pupil relationships, generosity in the appraisal of the behavior and motives of other persons, strong interests in reading and literary matters, interest in music and painting, participation in social and community affairs, early experiences in caring for children and teaching (such as reading to children and taking a class for the teacher), history of teaching in the family, family support of teaching as a vocation, strong social service interests . . ."[4]

Although one can indicate in a general way the characteristics of outstanding teachers, there is not necessarily an ideal facilitator equally effective with all learners. Rather, the effect of one individual upon another is a function of the personality structure of both individuals. Therefore, different kinds of facilitators affect variously different kinds of learners.

Although no one facilitator is ideal for all learners, the history of learning does provide examples of model teachers. One such model is Socrates. "Socrates remains our perfect model of the teacher. He was at home in the philosophy, science and literature of his age; he was a man among men . . . he loved young people . . . Socrates adapted himself to the capacity of each pupil; his good humour was unshakable; his manners were gracious even with cynics and fools; and he wore his superiority with humility. Above all things this is the truly religious man, dedicated . . . to the mission of leading youth toward the good life. He remains in his greatness the humble seeker after truth alongside those who know little but are capable of learning how to learn."[5]

Socrates was a model facilitator in that he did not indoctrinate but helped the learner to elicit and clarify his own question and to follow the argument where it led. Socrates believed that the learner must think for himself and find truth for himself; and if he seemed to be coming to error or delusion rather than to truth, he must simply be inspired to question more persistently and more profoundly. Socrates maintained this as the only way by which one could educate himself.

Although the learner is primarily responsible for educating himself, the facilitator's personality has a marked and measurable effect on the learner's growth, both academically and socially. Only the facilitator who is true to himself will be able to affect in a positive way the lives of the learners. This is so because growth is a natural process which requires that those who participate in it be true to their nature, be real, be authentic. Only an authentic person can assist in the natural process of growth which learning is. The learning process which is real affects the lives of the learners and facilitators in such a way that they are no longer the same for having touched by the other.

Much is required of one who would touch the lives of others and so affect upon them a permanent impression. It is a work of creation, the work of an artist. That is why the facilitator must possess a deep understanding of human nature and great skill in bringing it to perfection. "The material with which the educator works, which he must be able to mold in true creative fashion, is man himself, the masterpiece of Creation. It is man whom the educator must understand — man in his full scope and power — as a gardener wisely tends the rarest plants, from their first sprouting to the maturing of their fruit. The teacher must be capable of watching man's development, whatever direction it may take, whatever the circumstances. No profession on earth calls for a deeper understanding of human nature, nor for greater skill in guiding it properly."6

The facilitator's understanding of human nature and his skill in guiding it flow from his love for the learner; but before the facilitator can love the learner, he first loves himself. This self-love is not based on a selfish ego-centricity, but rather on integrity. The one capable of loving himself is an integrated person, a fulfilled person. The integrated person has a positive view of himself and of his world and accepts his identity within and his relation to the totality of his world. To love himself, as well as his world, is therefore, the only worthy human response. He perceives the good in himself and loves himself for what he is as well as for what he can become. Having an accurate perception of his real relationship to others and the world, the facilitator accepts himself as some one who is capable of genuine worth.

Because the facilitator is able to love himself, he is capable of loving the learner; and he does so honestly. This love is based first on a respect for the person of the learner. The facilitator respects the learner for who he is, a human person growing into completion, into wholeness. He respects the learner as a free and responsible being. Because of this respect for the learner, the facilitator provides opportunities through which the learner may exercise his responsibility and freedom and thereby come to maturity.

The facilitator who respects the learner and proves this by providing him freedom to be himself and to learn in his own way, also accepts him just as he is, realizing however, that he can become much more. But, the facilitator cannot know who the learner can become. He cannot know all of the possibilities which lie within the learner; therefore, he does not maintain an ideal of what he thinks the learner should be. The dangers inherent in maintaining an ideal have been expressed thus: "When we are working together for an ideal, for the future, we shape individuals according to our conception of that future; we are not concerned with the human beings at all, but with our idea of what they should be. The what SHOULD BE becomes far more important to us than what IS, namely, the individual with his complexities. If we begin to understand the individual directly instead of looking at him through the screen of what we think he should be, then we are concerned with what IS. Then we no longer want to transform the individual into something else; our only concern is to help him to understand himself, and in this there is no personal motive or gain . . . Ideals have no place in education for they prevent the comprehension of the present. . . . Is not the pursuit of a ready-made Utopia a denial of the freedom and integration of the individual? . . . Education in the true sense is helping the individual to be mature and free, to flower greatly in love and goodness . . . not . . . shaping the child according to some idealistic pattern . . . As long as education is based on cut-and-dried principles, it can turn out men and women who are efficient, but it cannot produce creative human beings. Only love can bring about the understanding of another."7

The facilitator does not impose himself, his ideas, or his feelings upon the learner; he only relates with who the learner is at each given moment, aware that changes constantly occur both within the learner and within himself. The facilitator realizes that both he and the learner are continually in the process of change and growth.

Therefore, their relationship also continually changes. At every given moment the facilitator learns who the learner is and accepts his realness. Through this respect and acceptance of the learner, the facilitator proves his love.

The facilitator's love is special and specific for each student. Since this love is personal, it touches what is most human about the learner; this is his freedom. The facilitator proves his love primarily by guiding the learner in the process of self-creation, which is fundamentally a process of growth in freedom. Therefore, the facilitator is one who, through his personal love for the learner, helps him realize his freedom.

Just as the facilitator's love helps the learner to be free, so too it promotes the growth to wholeness of the learner. Love develops wholeness because it does not impose limits. Love does not define a learner's potential; rather it acknowledges the open-ended possibilities of human creation. Love is the only power through which creation can occur.

Only the power of love can create positive growth in the learner. Only because of his love for the learner is the facilitator able to relate in a positive way with the child. Indeed, the child's basic motivation for learning comes from the realization that he is lovable and loved. Pestalozzi expressed a related idea thus: "Teaching, by itself and in itself, does not make for love, any more than it makes for hatred. That is why teaching is by no means the essence of education. It is love that is its essence. Love alone is the eternal effluvium of the divinity that is enthroned within us. It is the central point from which the essentials of education flow. Without love, neither the physical nor the intellectual powers of the child will develop naturally. That is only human." [8]

In addition to loving the learner, the facilitator also believes in him. Because he believes, he approaches life with the openness to receive whatever learning experiences life has to offer. This attitude of openness to life is based on the conviction that one is constantly changing and that life is a process. Therefore, the facilitator who believes is open-ended in his attitude and acknowledges that anything is possible.

Since the facilitator understands that learning is a natural growth process, he also has the optimism that its outcomes will have positive effects for the learner and for the facilitator. He believes that the learner can learn and grow and become a fully-functioning person. The facilitator proves that he believes this by the way in which he relates to the learner. That is he provides the learner with the opportunity to become all that he can become, and he assures the learner of success.

The facilitator's optimism leads him to favorable expectations regarding the learner. These favorable expectations can significantly affect the learning process. In his book, PYGMALION IN THE CLASSROOM, Rosenthal states: "It appears now that teacher's favorable expectations can be responsible for gains in their pupils' I Q's, and, for the lower grades, that these gains can be quite dramatic."[9] Rosenthal further states that ". . . findings lend support to hypothesis . . . When children are expected to gain intellectually they are more likely to be evaluated by their teachers against a higher standard."[10].

Finally, Rosenthal quotes from Shaw's PYGMALION these words of the flower girl: ". . . You see, really and truly, apart from the things anyone can pick up (the dressing and the proper way of speaking, and so on), the difference between a lady and a flower girl is not how she behaves, but how she's treated. I shall always be a flower girl to Professor Higgins, because he always treats me as a flower girl, and always will; but I know I can be a lady to you, because you always treat me as a lady, and always will."[11]

The facilitator who loves and believes in others, thereby assisting them in the process of achieving full growth potential, is himself a learner. He possesses the qualities which are characteristic of the learner; that is, he is open to experience and willing to be changed by it. He understands that like other learners, he is continually in the process of becoming fully-functioning. He is excited about learning and devoted to the discovery of truth. Because he seeks truth, he asks not who is right, but what is right.

Since the facilitator is a learner, he approaches the education process with the attitude of one who is himself teachable. That attitude is characterized by deep and honest humility. The humble facilitator acknowledges that in any situation he may be in error; however, he proceeds with the conviction that truth is attainable and that the act of discovery is possible for him. This realistic approach to knowledge and to the act of learning has been expressed thus: "The recognition that our truths are not copies of eternal realities but are human creations designed to meet human needs, puts one in a teachable frame of mind. And the discovery that thinking may be creative makes intellectual activity interesting."[12]

Part of the facilitator's intellectual activity consists in striving to know the learner. Because each learner carries within himself a part of the mystery of the universe, no one can ever know him completely. Yet the facilitator who is himself a learner unceasingly aims to know the student, not merely to know about him. He develops a sensitivity to what the learner needs in order to change and grow. He becomes increasingly aware of the interests, aptitudes, and aspirations of the learner. He develops an understanding of the learner's feelings.

This knowledge and understanding is gained by the facilitator through the mutual sharing of life's experiences in which facilitator and learner participate. The facilitator becomes a richer person as he encounters the uniqueness of the learner and as the learner becomes a part of him. He becomes richer in the very process of sharing himself with another.

As the facilitator respects and accepts each person entrusted to him, a greater unity of being as well as distinctness of identity is realized among all. As facilitator and learner get to know one another, they realize the communal dimension of their beings. They also realize that each of them is different from all others and that such uniqueness strengthens their sense of unity as well as their self-worth. The facilitator accentuates differences among the learners and lets them know that difference is good and desirable.

The facilitator not only knows and understands the learner, but he also seeks after truth in all its manifestations. Because he is an intellectually and experientially curious person, he applies himself diligently and with zeal in his search for meanings. He is an example of one who delights in learning, thereby being an important source of motivation for the learner.

The facilitator not only knows the learner and seeks after truth, but he also desires to learn wisdom, and for this he is an active listener. In his desire for wisdom he opens his whole being to all of life and receives the message of inner-relatedness which unites all people and stuff. The facilitator who seeks wisdom has learned to know himself, the learner, and the world, and sees a unity in all.

Not only is the facilitator aware of an inner-relatedness among all persons and things, but also he views life and the world from a perspective which is determined by a meaningful sense of values, and he knows no way to live except in keeping with his values. The greatest value is creation; the essential requirement for creation to happen is that one be free. This freedom consists basically in the power to determine one's response to life's situations. Since all of life's situations are a challenge to growth, the facilitator grows and thereby creates himself each time he makes a positive choice. He is free to use the opportunities presented by life to grow into a fully-functioning person; therefore, because of his freedom, he is an artist-creator of himself.

In relation to the learner the facilitator is an artist-creator who provides for the release of the creative powers of the learner and assists his complete evolution. Because he is an artist, the facilitator provides for the unfolding of the learner and assists him in the process of coming to maturity. As a true artist, the facilitator is honest with all with which he has been entrusted, for all art, to be significant, must be intrinsically honest.

Just as the artist sees more deeply into his times than other men, so too the learning facilitator who is an artist sees the act of facilitating more profoundly than teachers of lesser stature. He understands that where there is creativity, there is life. But one cannot plot life; one can only join in. It is the facilitator's role to follow the stream of the learner's creativity.

The facilitator's role in this process may be likened to that of a symphony conductor. "The skill a teacher requires is not far different from that required of a skilled symphony conductor: The sensitivity to the human instruments he deals with, the need to draw them out, whip them up, hold them back, bring out this voice and hush another, the rare ability to hear all the parts and yet retain a grasp of the larger whole toward which all are striving."[13]

The facilitator is also an artist-creator of ideas. He continually discovers new approaches to learning, new perspectives from which to view the familiar, and new insights into both past and present. He delights in considering ideas from yet another angle. The facilitator grows in greater depth of insight into people and situations and arrives at new thoughts. He who is an artist-creator of ideas expresses those ideas in new and untried forms. He is an artist with the material universe around him and a creator of newworks of art.

Through his experiences of loving, believing, learning, and creating, the facilitator grows in appreciation for himself, the learner, and his world. That is, he becomes more aware of the value of all persons and things. Because he values the world of people and of stuff, he also learns reverence for freedom, for persons who grow in freedom, and for whatever is an instrument of freedom. The facilitator who is free is pre-eminently qualified to assist another in the self-creation or learning process.

[1] Kahlil Gibran, *The Prophet,* pp. 56-7.

[2] Don Dinkmeyer, *"The C-Group Focus on Self as Instrument,"* *Phi Delta Kappan,* 52:10 (June 1971), p. 618

[3] Ibid., pp. 617-8

[4] David G. Ryans, *Characteristics of Teachers,* p. 366.

[5] E. B. Castle, *The Teacher,* p. 28

[6] Heinrich Pestalozzi, *The Education of Man: Aphorisms,* pp. 32-3.

[7] Juddi Krishnamurti, *Education and the Significance of Life,* pp. 21-3.

[8] Pestalozzi, p. 33.

[9] Robert Rosenthal and Lenore Jacobson, *Pygmalion in the Classroom, p. 98*

[10] Ibid., p. 107.

[11] Ibid., p. (183).

[12] Everett Dean Martin, *The Meaning of a Liberal Education, p. 102*

[13] Kenneth E. Eble, *A Perfect Education,* p. 108.

Chapter Three
The Learning Environment

The learning environment created by the facilitator who is a free and fully-functioning person is one in which the learner can grow to maturity because it is one in which the learner's nature is respected and opportunities for the fulfillment of that nature are provided. The learning environment is therefore a place of growth. It provides opportunities for growth to occur naturally, according to the learning needs of the student.

The opportunities for growth toward maturity are opportunities through which learning happens. These learning opportunities are based on learner needs. As indicated earlier, learner needs differ. No two people have identical needs and no two people learn alike. The best way for one to learn is determined by his unique personality. Experiences of adequacy, of personal fulfillment, cannot be provided in situations where all are treated alike.

As Richard Hostrop writes in his book, EDUCATION INSIDE THE LIBRARY-MEDIA CENTER, "In a hundred years of research into human learning only four axioms have proven true: (1) learning is facilitated if a person wants to learn (motivation); (2) learning is facilitated if a person knows what he is supposed to learn (expectations); (3) learning is facilitated if a person is actively involved in the learning exercise (participation): (4) learning is facilitated if a person has knowledge of results (feedback) — the sooner the better (reinforcement). All instructional systems need to incorporate those four axioms. Ancillary to the four axioms are two supportive techniques to facilitate learning: (1) the more of the five senses used in the learning process the greater will be the learning, and (2) learning will be enhanced if the learner or the learner's group is treated in a special way."[1] These axioms and techniques indicate the personal nature of learning and the need to respect the learner's responsibility for the process.

Since learning is facilitated if a person wants to learn, the learning environment is a place where student motivation stems from this desire. The character of the environment encourages the learner to become aware of his opportunity and responsibility for learning. The environment provides the tools of learning and permits him to use, explore, and discover as his needs and interests lead.

The student learns only what he is ready to learn. He is motivated to learn from his environment whatever has meaning or relevance for him. The learner is motivated when he sees the learning process as making a difference in his life, as affecting his ideas, opinions, feelings, and choices. Conversely, if a thing does not have meaning for him, he may remember something about it for a time, but he will not experience permanent learning . The learner will not be changed by any piece of information or an idea unless he has need of it, that is, unless he can integrate such a learning into his total learning structure.

Research also shows that learning is facilitated if a person knows what he is supposed to learn; therefore, the learning environment respects the expectations of students. Among these expectations is the student's right to expect that his needs will be met. He also expects that through the learning process his goals and means to them will be respected.

Learning is facilitated also when the learner is actively involved in the learning exercise, when he actively participates in the process. Education is understood here not as something done to the learner, but something which the learner does for himself. The learner takes an active part in those activities which have personal meaning for him. He does not simply follow directions and comply with what someone else tells him to do. He plans his own course, determines his own means, discovers his own line of action. He does not merely listen to a lecture prepared by someone else; rather, he does the research, he makes the discoveries, and thereby he is the learner.

Learner participation in the learning process means that the learning exercises are self-initiated, self-disciplined, and self-evaluated. A self-initiated activity is one based on learner needs and to which the learner makes the first response. A self-disciplined activity is one which the learner implements according to the structural requirements of his situation. The structural requirements are based on the nature of the learner and of his learning activity. Such an activity is not imposed, but rather it stems from the learner's needs. The result is neither license nor oppression, but the freedom to learn and grow according to his nature.

The learner not only initiates and disciplines his activities, but he also evaluates them. He evaluates his activities in terms of his expectations and in relation to his potential. He evaluates the outcomes in terms of the personal meaning they have for him.

Finally, research shows that learning is facilitated if the learner has knowledge of results through some form of feedback. The learner is aware of his progress. He knows that he is changing because of his responses to learning situations. Therefore, the learning environment provides opportunities for the student to observe these things for and about himself. It provides for a learning approach which satisfies this unique need.

A learning method which particularly respects the learner and his unique needs is that of the discovery method. The discovery method provides the learner with the opportunity to exercise his freedom. It gives him the opportunity to initiate, to pursue, and to evaluate in accord with his needs. It provides him the opportunity to learn how to learn.

The learner experiences participation in the learning process particularly through the discovery approach. Since the learner is by nature creative, he has a need to discover ideas for himself and by himself. He does not grow by being given another's idea to remember or to learn by rote; rather, he grows through the freshness of his own insights.

In the process of discovery the learner makes his findings his own. He integrates his findings into the world which he creates for himself. As he integrates, he realizes the power of discovery and the difference which it makes in his life. Also, he becomes more confident of his ability to discover, to learn, and to grow towards maturity.

The realization of his power of discovery motivates the learner to continue to ask questions and seek solutions. As he continues to question, he integrates his new discoveries with his person according to his own style. He develops a pattern of learning which is peculiar to him. The pattern of inquiry thus formed strengthens the learner's powers of retention and of thought.

Because this discovery approach meets his needs by contributing to his growth, it is a process of disciplined inquiry. Through it, the learner integrates what is required by the structural whole of his life and meaning. Thus integrated, all of his discoveries become a permanent part of him. That which is meaningful to the learner and that which he discovers through his own powers, become a permanent part of him.

The learner using the discovery approach is enabled to retain and apply material learned. He is able to make transferences.

Conclusions drawn from research comparing the directed discovery approach with that of direct and detailed instruction by a teacher indicate that "The directed discovery approach to teaching is superior to direct and detailed instruction with respect to retention of material initially learned as determined six weeks after instruction. The directed discovery method of teaching is more effective than the direct and detailed approach in enabling pupils to make wide applications of material learned to new and related situations, both at one and six weeks after instruction."[2]

The discovery approach to learning which is based on learner needs respects his freedom to learn how to learn. This freedom is also evident in the learning situation characterized as indirect. "Indirect teaching includes the behaviors of questioning, of accepting, clarifying or extending pupil ideas, of praising, and of accepting feelings. Direct teaching includes lecturing, giving directions, criticizing, and justifying authority."[3]

According to other studies "Indirectness of teacher behavior tends to be positively associated with achievement growth, favorableness of pupil attitudes and creativity growth. Teacher flexibility tends to be positively associated with achievement gain . . . several studies suggest that pupil growth increases as freedom and self-direction increase, but only up to a point . . . the point at which maximum growth takes place appears to be a function of the complexity or abstractness of the learning task —— the more abstract the task the greater the freedom which is optimal; the more concrete the learning, the greater the teacher control which is optimal."

Still other research indicates that when "The purpose of the learning experience is to exercise and to reinforce the learner in what may be called 'searching behavior' — — strategies of problem solving, divergent as opposed to convergent thinking, flexibility in thinking —— in essence, the characteristics of what is often labeled 'the creative person',"[5] discovery or guided discovery techniques are most appropriate.

When the learning process is understood as providing for the evolution of the creative person, the discovery approach would seem to be most appropriate. This approach respects the freedoms consistent with the learner's nature. However, as shown above, the indirect teaching method also promotes learner creativity.

A learning approach which promotes learner creativity is one in which the learner cannot fail. Such a fail-free approach is based on several concepts which aim to bring the learner and his environment together in such a manner that the learner can experience success. These concepts are: seeking, self-selection, and pacing.

"Seeking behavior is typical of the true learner in that such a person is naturally active and continually engaged in exploring the environment in which he exists. The learner naturally seeks for his environment those experiences which are appropriate to his maturity and his needs; on the other hand, that which is considered unmeaningful, even if judged on such a basis as lack of maturity, information, interests, or need, is ignored by the learner until he is capable of profiting therefrom. Self-selection, on the other hand, is characterized by the tendency of an individual to choose, on the basis of maturity and background, those activities for which he has a need. The third concept, pacing, involves both the learner and the teacher, for while the former will progress at a rate which is commensurate with his ability, the latter must be certain that materials are provided. The dual nature of pacing is evident when one realizes that just as a student will seldom challenge himself to greater effort unless he sees relationships, the teacher's role will be largely without purpose unless he arranges materials so the learner can manipulate them with clarity and meaning to himself."[6]

The learning environment which provides opportunities for seeking, self-selection, and pacing is one in which the learner experiences personal meaning and permanent changes. Because the learner is permanently changed by his discoveries within this environment, he expresses himself according to who he has become through them. The learning environment provides him opportunity to express himself, and in the process of self-expression he becomes ever more creative, releasing his energies within. The release of creative energies frees the learner, thus providing the basis for further thought, feeling, and insight.

The learning environment provides opportunities for the learner to exercise his thinking processes. Through these processes the learner forms and produces concepts and ideas. These processes require discipline and concentration. Most importantly, the ability to think requires freedom from fear and confusion. Thinking can happen only in a learning environment which is characterized as life -giving, free, and creative.

The learning environment also provides situations through which the learner realizes his sensible powers. He needs opportunities to free the powers of his senses, the power to see keenly, listen intently, and feel deeply. The learner needs to realize the rhythm of himself as a participator sharing the rhythm of the universe. He needs also to become intuitive and aware of all forms of life in his world and all aspects of life within him. All of these needs can be best met in a learning environment based on respect for learner needs.

The learning environment offers the learner the challenge to grow in his decision-making ability. This challenge is present when the learner is responsible for deciding the direction of his education. The learner who exercises this power to choose experiences a sense of security. He is free from fear of failure. He trusts his own experience and judgment. Such trust is the result of positive experiences in learning, particularly of positive experiences with other persons, such as learning facilitators. The learner, therefore, has a sufficiently strong self-concept to risk the chance he takes in assuming responsibility.

The power to choose is innate, it requires but exercise to bring it to fulfillment. In exercising this power the learner creates the highest form of art; that is, man in the process of using his responsible freedom. It is within the learning environment that the learner can bring to maturity this natural power.

The learning environment is a place in which the learner enhances his self-concept. The environment gives him opportunities for increasing consciousness and for becoming aware of the evolution of powers within him. As he grows in awareness of these powers, he realizes himself as a person-in-process. This realization enables him to see himself as having influence and even control over the material world. He sees himself as being of value for the world, as one who makes a difference. As a result his self-concept is enhanced.

The learning environment is one in which the learner can express the self he has become. He expresses himself through various means of communication. He speaks, writes, reads, performs, designs, draws, and paints; or he discovers any other way in which he can give authentic expression to the being that he has formed. The learning environment respects the need for such expression by providing opportunities for it.

The learning environment is a place in which the learner acquires increased knowledge of self. The learner acquires such self-knowledge through reflection on experience and especially through reflection on his responses. The learner needs, therefore, to have experiences which call for a response. He needs the opportunities for reflection which are provided by the learning environment.

Finally, the learning environment offers the learner opportunities to relate to the world. Such relationships happen through the learner's use of tools of learning and through his communication with facilitators and peers. These relationships also happen through the process of self-expression. In these ways the learner allows himself to touch and to be touched by his world. Also, he realizes his influence on the persons and stuff of his environment.

The learning environment in which the learner can relate to his world is a place in which his human nature is respected. It is, therefore, a place where people are valued over things, where creativity can fluorish, not being inhibited by undue concern for man-made rules, and where the learner's right to be a free and responsible individual is valued over all.

Since the learner is an individual, the learning environment is characterized as a place which fosters the learner's identity. In this environment he comes to know his uniqueness: who he is, that he is apart from others, that he shares a relationship with others. The environment fosters this identity through providing opportunities for communication, interaction, and cooperation.

The environment fosters identity by providing communication possibilities. Communication is a sharing of oneself with other persons and things. It is participating in the life which permeates the learning environment. Communication requires attentiveness and listening. It requires openness and receptivity to another —— whether person or thing. Finally, communication requires authentic self-expression. Through these processes of sharing, participating, listening, and expressing, the learner realizes his identity. The learning environment, therefore, provides for these processes.

The learning environment fosters identity through interaction. The learner interacts with other learners, with facilitators, and with tools of learning. He interacts by feeling, choosing, thinking, and other forms of behavior. His behavior interacts with the behavior of others by influencing other's behavior, which may in turn, affect his future behavior. Through his behavior and process of mutual interaction, the learner further realizes his identity.

Within the learning environment the learner also realizes his identify by working and playing cooperatively with others. He sees the value of his contribution to a team of workers, thinkers, and do-ers. He is aware of himself functioning as a member of a community of learners. Therefore, he values himself first for who he is, and also for what he can be and do for others.

In addition to being a place which fosters identity, the

learning environment is further characterized as one open to experience. The character of this environment encourages the learner to admit the untried and to try something new. It needs, desires, chooses, and risks the adventure of searching the unexplored and the undiscovered. It is a place permeated with new experiences. The learning environment is not only a place which provides for new experiences to occur, but it is a place characterized by trust of these experiences. An experience is trusted when it is accepted as having value in itself and as a valid basis for further exploration. The environment exudes confidence in the human ability to have meaningful experiences.

Finally, the learning environment is characterized by its being a place of respect for life lived as a process. It is for the learner an atmosphere in which life is accepted moment by moment as a process of change. In this atmosphere patience reigns supreme. Patience impregnates the atmosphere with the tranquility experienced in awaiting the outcomes of creative endeavor.

When life is lived as a process, learning, which is a creative endeavor, is valued because it is seen as a process of continuous growth. Learning is accepted as a natural expression of life and as the release of creative energies which create self and the world. It is valued because it satisfies a basic human need.

The learning environment is also characterized as a place in which life is accepted as a process through which the learner develops values. The development of values is possible in an environment in which the learner is exposed to alternatives and challenged to make choices from among them. He is able to choose intelligently because he sees values in relationship. In experiencing free and responsible decision-making the student learns to choose what is good and reject what is negative.

In this environment life is also experienced as a process through which the learner develops convictions. Immersed in learning resources representing diverse opinions and ideas, the learner reaches his own conclusions. These conclusions, however, are temporary, since all evidence is open-ended. The learner is not given answers to questions, but he discovers and explores for himself. Because of this approach, he learns to think. His convictions, having been arrived at through his own initiative and activities and for his own reasons, are firm, a permanent part of him; they have personal meaning for him.

Finally, in this learning environment, life is accepted as a process which develops the courage to be. The learner possesses the courage to be and to live his convictions. He expresses his convictions by his very being; he is not fearful. He lives in accord with what he considers to be authentic for him. He is integral, since his convictions and life style are in accord. Because he has formed his convictions based on internal motivation, they are a permanent part of him.

In summary, the learning environment may be described as a place

"Where human development in dignity and honesty is put first, and other goals subordinated to more realistic positions —
Where each child's spiritual integrity —— his right to be —— is recognized
Where his individuality is considered an asset rather than a liability
Where his genetic growth patterns are respected and used as a basis for teaching
Where he helps to purpose and to plan
Where he can act freely, knowing those around him accept him as he is
Where he can make an error —— or even do wrong, and not lose face thereby
Where he can grow each day and know that he is growing
Where he can hold his head up high and meet the others' gaze
Where he can make friends, enjoy other people, learn how to extend a hand to help
Where he can learn the warm flood of gratitude that comes from being regarded with warmth
Where he can venture into known worlds and stretch his wings to find new truths
Above all, where he can experience success in subject matter, human relationships and the discovery of self as a person of worth and dignity ——
In such an atmosphere, strong selves will grow, facilitated and tempered by the give and take, the struggle and the tolerance, the failure and the success, knowing that dignity which comes from being well loved and well respected."7

The learning environment discussed here can be the experience of learners at all stages of the learning process. A description of learning at several of these stages is considered in the following chapters.

[1] Richard W. Hostrop, *Education Inside the Library-Media Center,* p. 38.

[2] Willis E. Ray, "Pupil Discovery vs. Direct Instruction" *Journal of Experimental Education, XXIX* (March, 1961), p. 280.

[3] Robert S. Soar, "Research Finding from Systematic Observation" *Journal of Research and Development in Education, 4* (Fall, 1970), p. 117.

[4] Robert S. Soar, "Teacher Behavior Related to Pupil Growth" *International Review Of Education, 18:4* (1972), p. 522.

[5] Bert Y. Kersh and Merl C. Wittrock, "Learning by Discovery: An Interpretation of Recent Research" *The Journal of Teacher Education, XIII:4* (December, 1962), p. 467.

[6] Robert L. Curry and Gene D. Shepherd, "Learning in a Personalized Media Environment" *The Library-College Journal, 3* (Spring, 1970), pp. 29-30.

[7] Arthur W. Combs, *Perceiving Behaving Becoming,* pp. 232-3.

Chapter Four
The Library-College Concept

"The Library-College is an educational ideal based on the concept that the single most important instrument in the learning process is the library."[1] According to Library-College thought, "... the term 'Library' means environment. study tools, and personalized communitation; while 'College' refers to learning, self-directed study, and experimental growth. . .The hyphen in the term 'Library-College' signifies the interlocking nature of these elements."[2]

The interlocking nature of library and college is further indicated in the aim of this educational concept and movement. ". . . its aim is to show how the library can be a vital element at each level of every class in the curriculum. In doing this the Library-College is not pre-occupied with gadgetry, administrative routine, or narrow technical matters; rather, it seeks to find a new approach to methods of study in which the educational competence of subject-oriented librarians can be joined to the daily teaching efforts of classroom personnel."[3]

Through a new approach to methods of study, the Library-College concept provides for increased effectiveness of learning. Such effectiveness is realized through the combination of several elements which constitute the Library-College way. These elements include a library-centered learning environment, a mode of learning characterized by independent study, and a bibliographically expert faculty.

The library-centered learning environment includes the generic book and the bibliographic way. The generic book, a term used by Louis Shores, an originator of the Library-College concept, is defined by him as follows. "Briefly, the GENERIC BOOK, can be defined as THE SUM TOTAL OF MAN'S COMMUNICATION POSSIBILITIES. It includes all media FORMATS, SUBJECTS, and LEVELS. Under this definition, a 16 mm motion picture is just as much of a book as, for example, a collection of 32 or more pages of paper, bound or loose-leaf, consisting of printed reading matter or illustrations . . . Other formats of the GENERIC BOOK include, filmstrips, and transparencies; discs, tapes, radio transcriptions and videotapes; community resources — natural, social, human, programmed materials print, machine, and computer-assisted, as well as all kinds of print, and other sensory, and even extra-sensory media, . . ."4

A concept of learning which is library-centered provides the quantity and kinds of generic book commensurate with the needs of each learner. This learning concept assumes that these needs are different for each student. Through the use of the generic book, the individual differences in students can be matched with individual differences in media. Each student learns in his unique way through media most appropriate to his needs. Because the Library-College concept provides the learner with the generic book, it involves him in all of the communication possibilities; it meets his education needs and promotes effectiveness of learning.

Library-centered learning not only provides all possible tools of communication through the generic book; it also includes a bibliographic way or approach to learning. A bibliographic approach to learning provides the learner with access to the widest possible range of the literature of the subject. It does not limit to a prescribed reading list or to course requirements. It makes him responsible not to a course, but to all the subject matter of a field. It does not limit him to reading within a particular area or discipline. It does not limit him to a textbook which gives a one-sided view of the field of study with no sense of movement of thought in the field and which does not compare with those volumes which have been significant in the history of thought. It does not limit him to a textbook which gives predigested solutions and conclusions from which no significant learnings can be gained. Rather it opens to the learner the entire range of the literature of the subject, thereby extending the possibilities for seeing relationships, for breadth and depth of insight. In keeping with the generic book concept, the literature of the subject can be "read" through use of all of the media referred to above, including the printed word. With this approach, wide-ranging reading and thinking become natural, comfortable, an exhilarating and successful experience for the individual learner.

Through the bibliographic approach to learning, the learner becomes immersed in the literature of the subject and thereby encounters all possible points of view in relation to any subject. Since any author can offer only limited or particular views on a subject, the learner involved with the entire range of a subject's literature has the advantage of experiencing a breadth of view possible because of the library-centered, bibliographic approach to learning.

Viewed thus, the library does not support a curriculum; rather, it constitutes the curriculum. In fact, it can be the only true curriculum for learning, since unlike a specialized classroom collection, a textbook, or a reading list, the library collection represents a significant summary of the accumulated knowledge of the ages; it provides a reproduction of the world's thought.

The interdisciplinary nature of the bibliographic way offers the learner the opportunity to integrate knowledge and thus to achieve for himself a sense of order. This process of integration, made possible because of the learner's encounter with all of the resources of the library, is therefore a means by which the learner achieves a sense of unity within himself. As he sorts, criticizes, and evaluates the various opposing, conflicting, or substantiating ideas, opinions, and facts discovered through the generic book, the learner orders his own ideas and opinions and develops a unified perspective. He uses all possible learning resources, integrates these with himself, and determines an order for his life. This order is based on his values, which in turn affect his decisions, his behavior, and his ideas.

Because the interdisciplinary nature of library-centered learning brings the student into contact with various points of view, it encourages him to develop his powers of critical discernment and independent judgment and to respect these powers within himself. He learns to value all contributions to the world of thought and is not restrained by a deference to authorities which have been set up; rather, he learns to think for himself.

Since the bibliographic way is all-inclusive in its approach to the materials of learning, it provides the learner with the opportunity to, at least vicariously, experience all of the world. Immersed in subject matter representing divergent viewpoints, the learner freely follows any of the muses and realizes the excitement of personal discovery.

The interdisciplinary nature of the bibliographic way emphasizes ideas and problems rather than memorization of factual information. As the student moves among the disciplines, he encounters ideas which interrelate and problems in one discipline dependent for solution upon information and understandings from other disciplines. In the process of dealing with these ideas and problems, the student exercises his powers of thinking, discerning, and deciding. In other words, he develops his liberating qualities.

An approach to learning which develops liberating qualities is necessarily an individualized approach since each person's powers of thought, discernment, and judgment are unique. The learner becomes liberated and educated insofar as he perfects these qualities. An approach to learning which respects the learner's right to fulfillment in these ways and which respects the nature of the learning process is that which constitutes a second element of the Library-College way, namely, independent study.

Independent study is appropriate to a library-centered approach to subject matter. Library-centered learning provides the materials and resources, while the independent study approach involves the learner in determining his use of them. The learner determines his own goals and means. Also, he progresses according to his own needs. The independent study approach respects the personal freedom of the learner to learn in his own way.

The foundation of independent study is reading, and reading here means communication between the student and his environment through every existing medium. These media from which the learner reads may include a presentation, a discussion or other group activity. He may also "read" from a book, a tape, a film, or any other hardware. This approach to study is independent because it is done by an individual learner in keeping with his needs, interests, and creativity, regardless of whether the learning activities involve a single individual, a small or a large group.

The independent study approach provides the learner with the opportunity to grow in self-knowledge which is necessary in order to develop the discipline basic to learning how to learn. The process of learning how to learn is based on a knowledge of self and a self-discipline which are personal. Insights about the self gained in the process of learning how to learn continually change and develop. As the learner's self-knowledge deepens, he re-adjusts his goals and the behavior required to meet them.

In the process of learning how to learn, the student develops an understanding of his processes of thinking, sensing, and choosing. He develops an awareness of his own thinking process and of the insights which he receives. He realizes the creative process which occurs within himself and he becomes aware an awakened consciousness. Such processes occur during moments of concentration, of openness, and during an experience of freedom.

The student learns how to learn through using his senses, and he increases the power of his sensibility through his encounter with the wide variety of experiences available to him through the generic book. From among the many resources of the library, including books, art objects, laboratory specimens, tapes, and pictures, the learner is free to experience those things which have meaning for him. He does this in his own way because of the independent study approach.

The student learns how to learn through exercising and understanding the process of free choice. The student is free to choose, and he learns the responsibility which his freedom implies. He learns his values through his choices; and he learns to know himself through the values which his choices represent. In other words, the student learns the personal meaning of his choices.

The learner also comes to understand the process of decision-making among persons as he grows in awareness of the freedom enjoyed by others, of their values, and the extent of their decision-making ability. This interrelatedness among persons and their mutual responsibility to life's situations become significant learnings in the experience of the young learner.

Because the learner is free, only he can educate himself. In a very real sense, no one can teach him anything; but someone can give him the chance to learn. Teachers can offer, present, give, but only the learner's free response will result in a truly educated person, one whose creative energies have been released, and who has therefore changed. Since learning is an interior process of change and dependent upon the free responses of the learner, the student must be committed to the principle of full personal responsibility for his own education.

Because the student is exposed to a variety of learning resources through the generic book, and because he is free to make his own discoveries through independent study, he learns to respond to learning experiences which are meaningful to him based on his needs and interests. Since he is motivated to learn from all resources, he develops competency in an intelligent use of all tools of learning.

Having learned to consider all of the people and stuff of life as a learning resource, the learner develops an attitude of continual receptiveness, an openness to all that he encounters throughout life. He has become attuned and sensitive to opportunities. His approach to life's resources indicates this sensitivity, awareness, and competency.

The independent study approach provides the learner opportunity to develop competency in encountering life's challenges. It particularly develops competency in reading, as understood in its broadest sense; in listening, understood as a most intense activity; in self-expression. The learner develops his inherent creativity in these areas in accordance with his own needs.

Since education is a process of personal growth arising from a learner's needs, he himself must assume the initiative in defining his goals or problems. The learner's goals are unique; only he can really know what they are. Only he can define his expectations. No one can tell another person what he needs to know. A teacher cannot tell a student what his needs are. A facilitator can guide, encourage, and otherwise assist; but his primary role is to cooperate with the free spirit which prompts the learner to initiate the release of his creative energies thus educating himself.

Just as the learner's goals and problems are unique, so too are his methods in investigating these problems. Therefore the student assumes the initiative in selecting his methods of investigation and in conducting a critical exploration. Only the learner knows himself well enough to determine the means he will use in attempting to solve a problem. These means represent the way in which he learns, and they are based on his personal potential; therefore, the student selects methods appropriate to his nature at any given moment.

The student also assumes the initiative in reporting findings. The learner reports those findings which have value and significance for him. Findings have significance for him insofar as they are relevant to his search, to his goal, to his problem, to his need. The learner reports his findings in a way appropriate to these elements. Having reported his findings, the learner evaluates these on the basis of his personal, unique sense of values. He determines the significance and value of his findings relative to who he is and who he has become.

The independent study approach to learning also encourages the student to assume initiative in evaluating the activities which lead to a conclusion. Since the student is primarily responsible for selecting and carrying out the activities, and since these are based on his needs and goals, he is most able to evaluate these activities in relation to their having met his needs and accomplished his goals.

These activities may be either internal or external. An internal activity is one which occurs within the individual. It refers to a line of reasoning pursued, to the development of memory, of will power or powers of concentration. Only the learner who is conscious of these powers within him is capable of evaluating the use of them, therefore evaluating them as activities implemented in arriving at a conclusion.

External activities include all of the sensible actions carried out in the process of arriving at a conclusion. These include: reading, viewing, listening, performing, speaking, etc. Since the learner is the principal agent in this action, he assumes the initiative in evaluating the various activities; only he can evaluate the activities in relation to his needs and purpose.

The Library-College way of learning includes the idea that "each one teach one". Each student shares something of what he has learned with another student, and in this mutual exchange both are motivated and stimulated by the other. Since one learns effectively in the process of teaching or telling someone else, this technique of having a pair of students assist one another promotes the learning of both. Since the influence of the peer group is so strong among young people, the each one teach one idea channels this very real potential for a learning influence.

In addition to students assisting one another according to the idea of each one teach one, a bibliographically expert faculty also assists in the learning process. The Library-College, library-centered, independent study approach to learning requires a bibliographically expert faculty. A learning facilitator who is bibliographically expert is one who values earning resources, who reads widely and wisely, and who interprets honestly. Such a faculty is required for a learning process which includes the generic book and the bibliographic way. The bibliographically expert faculty includes teachers and librarians whose functions are integrated since all of them are competent in locating, using, and evaluating learning resources in their variety of formats, and both teachers and librarians are competent in assisting the student in these same ways.

The bibliographically expert faculty has knowledge of the generic book, of its purpose, its potential, its value as a learning resource. He knows how to read and interpret not only the printed page, but all forms of the generic book. Because he has knowledge of the relative values of learning materials, the bibliographically expert teacher uses original sources rather than second or third hand information whenever possible.

In a library-centered, independent study approach to learning, a bibliographically expert faculty serves as a facilitator of learning, as a resource person, a counsellor, and a scholar. As a facilitator the faculty member makes the learning process as simple, natural, and uncomplicated as possible for the learner. The learning process is facilitated insofar as all elements which constitute the process are based on student needs and understood as interrelated with all other parts and therefore related to the whole. In this way the entire process becomes one structured whole and possesses the freedom natural to it.

The faculty member also serves in the capacity of a resource person. As such he possesses within himself a wealth of knowledge, understandings, ideas, and wisdom. However, he seldom dispenses information or ideas, nor does he dictate opinions; rather, he suggests approaches and offers the learner guidance as the situation requires.

If the faculty member uses the lecture, he does so sparingly and mainly for purposes of inspiration. The lecture may have had its merits before the invention of the printing press, but nowadays when books, and the generic book, are readily available for the student to read, why lecture to him? The student can read material equivalent to that of a teacher's lecture in one-third of the time he spends listening to it. In addition, when the student reads, he is more involved than when he listens; plus he can comprehend more difficult material through reading than through listening. So why use the student's time for something he can learn more effectively by himself?

Finally, the lecturer's method of research, the work he does in preparation for a lecture is work which rightfully belongs to the student. In the process of doing this research, real learning can occur; while in listening to a lecture and taking notes on it, the pupil may practice mere memorization.

Another function of the facilitator is to serve as a group leader. In this capacity the faculty member is able to function effectively as a member of a team. He understands the process of group dynamics and helps a group of learners to interrelate, to cooperate, and to function harmoniously. Thereby, each group member is enabled to benefit from the insights shared among the whole group. Also, new ideas emerge, new freedoms are realized, new awarenesses develop in the non-threatening atmosphere provided by the group leader. In such a situation each participant is free to create and express himself.

The independent study approach to learning requires a bibliographically expert faculty who serves as a counsellor. In this capacity he needs a knowledge of students, an understanding of anda sensitivity to the needs and interests of the learner. This awareness of the learner is necessary in order for the teacher to assist him in matching media with his unique needs and goals.

As a counsellor the teacher advises, suggests, recommends, and otherwise assists the learner in realizing his creativity. He does not dictate, threaten, impose, but offers the student opportunities and situations in which he can learn how to learn. He expresses his enthusiasm for the learning which results and assures the learner of success. Such assurance is based on the learner's natural growth process; and according to this view, no learner can fail.

As a counsellor the teacher possesses the ability to communicate with the students. This communication includes a sharing of ideas, opinions, and feelings among learners and facilitators. The sharings lead to a recognition of common ideals and aspirations and to some degree of community life shared by all.

The faculty serves as an example of scholarship for the learner, as one intent on the pursuit of learning, both as a generalist and as a specialist. As a generalist the bibliographically expert faculty member has a broad, general background from which to draw. He recognizes the value of the literature of many subjects. He is broadly educated and aware of the philosophy and major concerns of other disciplines. As a specialist he has a penetrating insight into a subject area and can offer in-depth knowledge of his chosen specialty. He is an expert in his own field.

The library-centered, independent study approach, facilitated by a bibliographically expert faculty, results in an atmosphere of colleagues working together in the quest for knowledge, growth, and wisdom. This atmosphere is marked by intellectual excitement, delight and wonder at new discoveries. This atmosphere is possible because the faculty too capable of asking questions and searching for answers. Therefore, the faculty participates in search and synthesis with the students. In this type of situation, all participants whether facilitators or students, are learners.

Since the Library-College idea would have a situation in which all, children, youth, and adults, are learners; the idea of learning as a life-long opportunity receives new emphasis. The exemplars of life-long learning are the faculty. They continually strive to know the dynamics of learning. Through their inquisitive nature, independent thinking, and intellectual courage and initiative, they exemplify the truly educated person. Through their responses to life's learning situations and opportunities, they indicate to the younger learner the almost unlimited possibilities for growth available for one who has the courage to be.

Finally the bibliographically expert faculty is also continually open to experimentation with the untried and has a capacity for educational innovation. He has developed this attitude of openness because he realizes life as an unfolding, evolving process and sees himself as a part of it. He attempts a little more than he can do, and he works at being more than he is. He sees value in trying the untried and accepts open-ended possibilities with an attitude of hope. With this hopeful attitude the learning facilitator approaches the challenge of providing opportunities for the release of the creative energies of the learner. This challenge can be met through the library-centered and independent study approach of the Library—College concept.

[1] Howard Clayton and Robert T. Jordan, "Library-College" in *The Encyclopedia Of Education*, p. 608.

[2] Howard Clayton, *Learning Today*, 7:1 (Winter, 1974), p. 47.

[3] Clayton and Jordan, p. 609-10.

[4] Louis Shores, *Library-College USA:* Essay on a Prototype for an American Higher Education, p. xi.

Chapter Five
A Library-Centered Approach
to Learning in the
Junior High School

The library-centered approach to learning offers numerous excellent opportunities for learner growth. This is so because it respects the learner as he is with his peculiar needs, desires, and goals. Also, it accepts learning as a natural process of growth required for the learner to become mature.

The learner in the junior high school is on his way toward maturity. This chapter discusses some possibilities of the library-centered approach in assisting him in that process. However, this approach to learning is not peculiar to a particular grade or age level; rather, some of its possibilities are described here simply as examples of an approach which may be applicable throughout the educational system and with learners of all ages.

A library-centered approach in the junior high school places the learner in the midst of a wide variety of learning resources. The resources include a variety of media, including books, periodicals, recordings, projections; in fact, the entire range of the generic book as described previously.

This variety of media meets the need of the student who learns best by silent reading, of the one who comes to greater understanding through a visual representation of an object or an idea such as offered by a film or filmstrip, as well as of the student who learns more effectively when listening to a tape or other recording. By offering this variety of learning media, the library-centered approach respects the individual learning needs of all learners as well as of each learner at any particular time, since one may at one time prefer the use of audio aids while at another time one may prefer the silent use of the printed page. With this approach all of the senses are involved in the learning process as the learner listens, views, and in other ways experiences through the tools of learning.

Not only does the library offer a variety of forms of media; but it also offers a wide range of media. Its collection includes items ranging from those requiring the simplest to the most complex comprehension. Thus, for example a library collection for junior high students may range in reading level from grade three to eleven, or the range may be even wider. Within such a collection the learner is able to find materials which meet his present ability to read and understand. Situated in such an environment, the learner is encouraged to challenge himself to master increasingly complex material.

The variety of media refers not only to the various forms and levels of learning tools, but also to the extensive coverage of disciplines. That is, learning resources on every subject can be found within the library, thus providing for an interdisciplinary approach to learning. From among these various resources, the learner is able to find material which meets his needs and interests and from which, therefore, he will be able to learn.

Any one discipline, as for example, language arts, includes a variety of subject areas. These subjects include folk literature, puppetry, animal stories, mythology, poetry, historical novels, and biography. When these subjects are seen along with the numerous subjects of other disciplines, the result is an almost endless list of topics from which the learner may choose. Because of the library-centered approach, he will be able to find forms of media, levels of comprehension, and subject areas appropriate to his needs.

The learner's approach to these learning materials is not according to the dictates of a teacher, but rather according to learner needs. Thus he is not limited by specific requirements imposed by another, but he is free to choose his own direction. The learner decides with what subject area he will begin his pursuit, and he designs his individual course of study for it. This course of study, based as it is on his needs, indicates his goals and means to them. It may be so specific as to include a time-table of his activities. It may also provide for a progress record as well as for methods and results of evaluation. Most importantly, this course of study is flexible so that it can be adjusted to meet the changing needs of the learner.

The corollary of the library-centered approach is seen, therefore, to be independent study. The essential element of independent study is that the learner freely choose his own learning path. As a result of this free choice, a learner may be the only one in the school who chooses to read in a particular subject, or he may be the only one to express himself through a particular medium.

In the course of his independent study the learner in a junior high school participates in a variety of activities. These activities include reading, speaking, writing, discussing, researching, planning, evaluating, studying, presenting projects, using audio-visual materials and creating original learning materials. Since some of these activities involve shared participation, the young learner has the opportunity of meeting a need particularly crucial to his age group. That is the need for acceptance and approval by peers. Therefore, through the independent study approach, the learner is able to meet his needs as an individual learner who is a member of a society of learners.

As an example of how this approach may proceed, consider the case of the young learner who wishes to explore the area of folk literature. He is not limited by a teacher's reading list on the subject, but is free to pursue the study in the manner which he feels necessary in order to satisfy himself. The learner may choose, therefore, to read, view, and listen to folk literature for a few days, for several weeks, or even for a month or more. The young learner who pursues the study of folk literature does so at his own pace. He does not feel undue pressure in an attempt to keep up with others who read or comprehend more quickly, nor is he restrained by others who progress more slowly than he. Rather, he is free to read and reread, view and re-view, listen and listen again, scan, peruse, digest, and assimilate in keeping with his own needs.

The independent study approach, centered in the library, frees the learner to study folk literature in his own way. His way may be to listen to folk tales on tape, to view a filmstrip while listening to a recording, or to read about folk literature silently. He may even do extensive research on it, using encyclopedias, other reference books, magazines, and various audio-visual resources.

In his study of folk literature the learner may draw upon resource persons within or outside of the school setting. These may include persons with a particular expertise in the folk literature of a specific group of people or area. Perhaps a resource person has visited a geographic area and can offer information, personal impressions, or ideas about the subject not readily available in any other form.

After the learner has explored the area of folk literature, he may wish to express his findings through an art or craft project. Such expressions may include any form of communication: writing an essay, a poem, or a narrative story; giving an oral presentation such as an original skit or reading; composing a booklet of original writings and/or drawings; making a collage or other art piece; using audio-visual materials such as tapes and slides to present a program; or any other creative form of communication through which the learner can share with others something of his discoveries and thereby of himself.

Since the need for peer group acceptance is so strong among junior high students, several of them may decide to work cooperatively on some aspect of folk literature, thus providing mutual encouragement and support. They may decide to do a joint project to which each student contributes a part. For example, they may compare the folk literature of several peoples of the world, each student being responsible for research on the literature of a particular people. Their project may include combining their discoveries into some form of presentation to a larger group.

Whatever the activity chosen, the learner proceeds in his own way, using as much or as little time as he needs to complete his creative expressions. It is a distorted view which assumes that each student, working in his chosen area, needs exactly the same amount of time as all other students to make personal, meaningful discoveries and to create his own expression of them. The process of creation is personal, as is the created object; therefore, the learning process through which creation occurs provides the learner with the freedom required by creativity.

When the learner's interest in a topic wanes, he moves on to a different subject area, since no significant learning can occur without the motivation of interest. He may find, after a few days, that this subject does not meet his expectations and satisfy his needs for now. Having learned this about himself by himself, he leaves the study of folk literature, perhaps until a later time in his life, but leaves it without disliking it or having a negative attitude toward it. Since it was his to freely choose, it is for him to freely reject. Since this particular subject had not been imposed on him by a teacher, he does not cast it off with disdain, but with the attitude that someday, when he is ready for it, he will return to the study of it.

The learner's freedom includes his responsibility to choose his learning path. This path originates with the learner's interest. From within the discipline of language arts this may mean that the learner will choose to study a topic of special interest to this age group, namely, that of animals. The learner may even limit his study to that of a particular kind of animal, as for example, dogs.

Since printed matter is a basic means to learning, the student begins by searching for books about dogs. In his search for books on this topic, the learner encounters various tools of learning. Among these is the library card catalog. The student encounters the card catalog because his interest motivates him to do so; therefore, he is ready to learn how to use it. He discovers the subject cards for dogs and the various subdivisions of that main topic. He learns to distinguish books of dog stories from those dealing with factual information on habits and behavior of dogs. He finds that a cross-reference card directs him to books on animals, books which deal with dogs as a part of a larger classification.

The learner finds too that besides locating an animal book through the subject cards of the catalog, he can do so also through title and author cards. If, for example, he has read a dog story which he very much enjoyed, he may wish to read another book by the same author. Again, his personal needs and personal interest motivate him to further discoveries about this learning tool, discoveries which become a permanent part of him because they arise from within him.

Because of his internal motivation the student readily learns the meaning of all the information on the catalog card. He learns the use of the classification symbol in locating a book in the library, and he learns to read the descriptive cataloging. Having this ability, he is able also to prepare a bibliography of his own. This process too will have personal meaning for him because it is initiated and continued by him in accord with his needs and interests.

In addition to using the card catalog in his search for books, the learner uses it also in his search for audio-visual materials. Here too he learns the meaning of classification symbols which direct him to the location of materials, and he learns to read the descriptive notes on the catalog card. These may assist him in determining the use he will make of a learning item.

Through the cataloging and classification system of the library-media center, the learner becomes aware of the relationships among various media, of the uses of media, of the ways in which they complement other media, and of the ways in which they can assist him in arriving at understandings. In the process of using these various learning resources, he is open to receive insights into ways in which he can create with media in giving expression to his discoveries.

Besides reading books on the learner's chosen topic, in this case, dogs, he may also read magazine articles; and in his search for pertinent articles, he encounters another learning tool, namely, the guide to periodical literature. Of particular value to the junior high school student may be a subject index to magazine articles. Again, as in the case of books and materials, the learner who is free to choose his own learning path, is by that fact, readily motivated to grasp the means to his self-chosen end. He is ready to learn how to read an entry in a periodical index. Such learning has personal meaning for him at this time; it is relevant to his search.

The young learner may discover other learning materials in his search. In his discovery he learns how to use various books in the reference section of the library. Here we may encounter specific facts and detailed information not available elsewhere. Pamphlets and picture files provide still other material. The degree of sophistication in library use depends upon the individual learner, but with this library-centered, independent study approach, the possibilities are almost limitless. Such an approach provides opportunities for the release of creative energies in ways discoverable only by the young learner in the process of growing toward maturity.

The young learner whose interest in animals leads him to the tools of learning, to a wide range of learning materials, to a variety of formats and media, and who realizes his freedom to choose from among these, experiences something of the wholeness of learning. Such wholeness arises from the learning situation which provides opportunities for personal meaning through personal discovery.

The young learner experiences wholeness in this learning process because he is involved in the activities of centering, structuring, and discovering. He centers himself in the midst of learning resources and realizes himself in relationship to them. He centers his learning needs, interests and motivations within himself and sees them in relation to his creative potential. Experiencing himself as central in the learning process and aware that all centers on his freedom, he realizes also a structure to the entire process. He experiences a meaningful relationship among all elements of the learning process and sees all as part of a whole. Within this whole the learner makes personal discoveries and integrates all elements of the learning process within him.

The young learner who is free to make his own discoveries can, therefore, specialize and generalize according to his needs. He can concentrate on the study of folk literature, animals, or any other topic until he becomes an adolescent master of the material; or his reading on any topic may serve as a springboard to further interests and pursuits.

What a contrasting experience for the student who learns the library skills, such as the use of the card catalog and the periodical guide, within the context of a personal, meaningful, self-chosen, process vis-a-vis that of the student, who as a member of a class of twenty-five or more students, is given a routine presentation on these tools by a librarian or teacher. In the latter case, the presentation must of necessity be so general as to be nearly meaningless to most students. In the latter case the teaching is imposed from without; it does not arise from the learner's need or interest. Even the student who receives the librarian's individual attention with the use of the card catalog in doing an "assignment" is not learning as a free person, since the assigned work is some one else's idea. Only in the former situation is the learner ready to receive information and understandings because only in a self-chosen situation, structured to meet his needs, can he experience personal meaning. Only in such a whole situation can learning through library tools be a part of his discovery. Only then is the use of the learning tool integrally related to the student's learning.

This kind of experience results in organic learning. Organic learning flows from the learner's own needs and interests. it requires the learner to draw upon his own resources, make his own discoveries, and progress in his own way and at his own pace. Organic learning requires that the learner follow his own inspirations and thereby receive his own insights. Because this learning is organic, it is permanent.

Although the independent study approach provides for organic learning and is thereby individualized, it does not mean that the learner's activities are carried out alone at all times. Nor does he pursue his studies without regard for others. Rather the junior high school student needs to learn social responsibility through working with others and sharing learning resources and time with them. Because at this age level the learner depends heavily on the approval of peers and is greatly influenced by them, it is an ideal time in his life to deepen awareness of social responsibility.

The independent study approach encourages the young learner to share his time and himself with others. That is, he may work with another or in a small group for some part of a language arts project. Several students may do a joint project on puppetry. They may assist one another as they prepare for a group presentation. They may evaluate together their efforts toward presenting a program. They may share with one another the expressions of their creativity. They may make positive suggestions to one another, mutually encouraging one another to continue to discover, pursue, and create; thereby, they reveal their interest in one another's work. In these ways the students work independently as a group rather than as an individual.

The young learner shares library-media center resources with other learners. He keeps in his possession only those materials which he needs for the immediate time being, and he returns borrowed library materials promptly. Thus all of the holdings in the collection are more readily available for all. Because of the independent study approach, there is not a heavy demand on any one kind of material at any one time. For example, while one student may be pursuing the study of folk literature, another may be reading about animals. And while one is listening to a tape on mythology, another may be creating his original art project based on an historical novel. Since the students are not limited to course requirements, but may explore throughout the entire area of language arts and even in other disciplines, no one is frustrated by inability to procure learning resources appropriate to his needs.

Also, the students are not limited to the holdings of the school library, but may use any public library, bookstore, television program, or resource person from within or outside of the school. Indeed, the whole world becomes a learning center from which the learner may draw, relate, and integrate into his study.

This library-centered, independent study approach to learning meets the specific needs of the junior high school student. One of these needs is that of creating his individual uniqueness through the release of his creative energies. This need is met through the learning approach which respects the individual's freedom to respond to tools of learning according to his needs and interests. This learning approach provides the learner with the opportunity to exercise his innate freedom. It does so by freeing the learner to progress at his own pace and in his own way as determined by internal motivation.

The junior high school learner has a strong need to be self-confident. This self-confidence translates into trust of himself and of his own experiencing. Such trust arises from positive experiences, that is, experiences for which the learner himself set the stage and from which he received new insights.

Such experiences are an outcome of the library-centered independent study approach. In this learning approach, the learner determines his own goals and the means to them. Because his goals are self-made and in accordance with his needs, and because the means to them are self-selected, the learner can experience only success. Even if he does not attain a particular goal, or if he neglects a particular means, the total outcome remains a learning experience. He may not have achieved specifically what he set out to do, but because the process he followed was one of discovery and because it freed him to learn how to learn, he will have received greater self-understanding and greater understanding of the learning process.

During this learning process, the student does not suffer the frustration of the student in a teaching-centered or subject-centered situation. In those situations the teacher imposes information and ideas, and if the student fails to memorize this material within a given period of time, he may indeed fail. Failure in those situations is without compensation. Those approaches simply refuse the student the opportunity for permanent growth, for learning how to learn.

In addition to the need to be his unique self and the need for self-confidence, as mentioned above, the learner at this age level also needs to continue to read. The library-centered approach is ideal for meeting this learner need because it does not limit him to a teacher's bibliography but leaves him free to choose his own reading from among the thousands of volumes provided by a library. Being free to choose, the student learns to choose, and having learned to choose, he will continue to exercise the freedom to read.

The need to read includes not only the need to read the printed page but also to "read" recordings, films, filmstrips, slides, and other audio-visual materials. In fact, this need to read may be extended to include the need to understand all of the signs and symbols usually encountered when living in society. The ability to read the signs in one's world is part of the growth process or learning.

Another need of the junior high school student is that of being able to communicate effectively, and for this need to be realized, he develops basic language skills. He learns the language techniques of writing and speaking through constant exercise in these skills. The learner exercises his writing skill most effectively as he writes about things and ideas of interest to him. Therefore, his topics of written work often follow from the topics about which he reads. Just as he chooses his reading, so too he chooses the topics on which he writes. As the student exercises this language skill, he gains competence in expressing himself and in communicating effectively.

The young learner in the junior high school needs also to develop personal responsibility. He develops this by being trusted with responsibility. He is responsible for his daily use of time and of resources, and he may be asked to account for these through the keeping of a daily log of his activities. Such a log may be evaluated by the learner and facilitator at regular intervals. In this way the learner continually evaluates his responsibility.

This personal responsibility is closely related to the social responsibility of the learner. Social responsibility includes the learner's awareness of his responsibility as he shares time, resources, and himself with others; and as he respects other's needs, goals, and places of study.

The learner needs also to develop self-direction. This is realized as he freely, with the assistance of a facilitator, chooses his own learning path, his goals, and his resources. He does not depend upon a teacher to tell him what to do, but he learns to initiate his own discoveries and to follow through according to his own plan. From among the various disciplines the learner determines the specific topics he will pursue as well as the way in which he will proceed.

Finally, the learner has a need to develop his personality through creativity. He does this as he experiments with creative uses of resources, including various media, and as he creates means of self-expression through them. While the learner satisfies this immediate need, he also prepares himself for creative use of leisure both now and for the future.

All of these learner needs are basic to human nature. All of them need to be fulfilled if the learner is to grow toward maturity, since they are essential to that growth process. These needs of the junior high school learner can be met in the ways described above through the independent study approach to learning.

What is the role of the teacher and of the librarian in this library-centered, independent study approach to learning? Briefly stated, the roles of both become essentially one. That is, both serve as facilitators of learning, and in this capacity they assist the learner in his process of discovery, of change, of growth toward maturity. They do this in various ways.

The facilitator provides the learner with an abundance of learning resources. Such an abundance includes the entire range of library-media center materials as well as any others which are available from homes, public libraries, resource persons, and any other part of the learner's environment. These resources include books, periodicals, and audio-visual items as well as items for art and craft projects. Items falling into this latter category may be considered "junk" by some, but when used by a creative young learner, these things serve as an original means of self-expression. "Junk" thus challenges the imagination of the young artist. All of these materials form a rich smorgasbord from which the learner may draw.

Besides providing materials for the present time, the facilitator is also alert to possible learning materials to be procured for the future. Thus the facilitator never becomes complacent in having once and for all supplied resources, but he remains open to future possibilities for new items to be provided and for new, creative uses of the present library-media center collection. This collection is, therefore, not rigidly fixed, but is in a constant state of flux.

In addition to providing learning resources, the facilitator assists the learner in the use of these materials. Teachers, as well as librarians, are bibliographic experts who read widely and wisely and lead the learner among the entire range of resource materials available through an interdisciplinary approach to learning. The facilitator knows the learner and can effectively match learner with learning tools. The facilitator assists the learner in the use of library tools as, for example, the card catalog, guide to periodicals, and other bibliographies. He does this at the time the learner experiences a specific need to know, not as a matter of mere routine. In these ways, and others, the facilitator shares in the learning activities of the student.

Besides providing learning resources and assisting students in the use of them, the facilitator gives special help as needed. He gives special help to the learner who has not experienced the freedom to learn throughout his years at school. The facilitator gives some direction to the student who has not acquired a measure of self-discipline, thus helping the student learn to channel his freedom toward responsibility and growth. The facilitator assists the student in formulating realistic goals for himself, if the student has not yet learned to set his own goals because he had always been subject to the plan of a teacher. In order to help in these ways the facilitator is sensitive to the specific needs of each learner.

All needs, whether common to all learners or specific to some, are met only in a non-threatening learning environment. Therefore, a further responsibility of the facilitator is to create such an atmosphere. In a non-threatening atmosphere the learner's energies are not wasted on his setting up of self-defenses, but are released for creative uses. In this learning environment the learner does not fear, because he trusts. Having dispelled student fears and earned the student's trust, the facilitator can open honest discussion which is basic to the authentic communication which learning requires.

A final, though none the less important responsibility of the facilitator is to give the learner encouragement and to assure him of success. The encouragement and assurance prompt the learner to meet his goals. Since the learner's ultimate goal is growth, and since that goal is a natural result of the learning process described here, the learner will meet his goal and will thereby experience a marked degree of wholeness.

The wholeness possible for a learner in a library-centered, independent study approach to learning is not possible for a student in a teaching-centered or a subject-centered approach. Such wholeness is not possible for many reasons, the most obvious being the use of the lesson plan common to these other approaches.

A lesson plan is a teacher's plan. Therefore, it cannot meet the learning needs of even one learner. It cannot assist one learner in the process of growth which of its nature is personal and therefore meaningful only when experienced internally by the learner, being based on his needs. Any plan for learning must of necessity be initiated and implemented by the learner; otherwise "learning" remains mere short-term and superficial memorization of information.

The teacher's lesson plan, based on the teacher's knowledge of subject matter, discourages the student from exercising his freedom to learn according to his nature, and it prevents him from assuming the responsibility for his own education. The lesson plan denies the learner the right to learn how to learn.

Noy only does the lesson plan thwart the growth process, but it fails in lesser ways as well. One lesson plan cannot meet the unique learning needs of twenty-five or more students all of whom learn at a different pace and in a different way. The lesson plan can only be a part of an indoctrination process in which the teacher aims to transfer a set amount of information from a book or from his mind to the mind of the pupil. This is usually done in the hope, on the part of both pupil and teacher, that the former will retain the information at least until after the test. The "poor" pupil is likely to forget too much too soon. However, such subject-oriented instruction cannot compare with the library-centered approach, if it can be considered education at all.

Among the functions of the facilitator, therefore, that of imposing lesson plans is not to be named. Rather, as indicated above, the facilitator takes his cue from the innate and boundless creative spirit of the learner. His function is to flow with that stream of creativity, not against it. As facilitator he nurtures the creative process, and through the library-centered, independent study approach to learning, he provides for the evolution of the creative person.

Chapter Six
Learning in the
Primary School Library

The child who enters the primary school has already spent five or more years discovering the world. In this process of discovery he has seen, listened to, touched, and in other ways sensed the world of his environment. He has experienced a relationship with the various and multitudinous objects which surround him. He has also experienced insights into how things are put together and how they come apart. He has assembled a picture puzzle and dissected a toy telephone. In addition, from a very young age he has experienced insights into human relationships; he has observed how the people around him relate with one another and with their environment, what he must do to get their attention, and which of his behaviors please and which displease the people whose world he shares.

The child learner has made his discoveries independently. He has not had to keep pace with children who learn more quickly than he, nor has his progress been hindered by those who learn more slowly. His learning rate has not been determined by the presence of other learners. Rather, he has been free to discover at his own pace and in his own way.

The pre-school child has discovered in his own way because he has not been forced to follow someone else's lesson plan. He has not been told what to discover or how to discover; rather, he has been free to follow the natural course of his curiosity. He has exercised freedom in choosing from his environment those things from which he would learn. He has decided which object he would pull out of his toy box to satisfy his interest and need of the moment, and he just as freely cast it aside when he no longer learned from it. He has learned naturally from the ordinary situations in his life and freely accepted or rejected whatever met or failed to meet his expectations. Because the pre-school child has discovered freely in accord with his interests and needs, he has, by age six, acquired a vast amount of information and various kinds of understandings. Also, because this discovery process has had personal meaning for him, the effects of his discoveries are permanent.

Because the pre-school child's approach to learning is characterized as free, it is also structured. This free, yet structured approach is evident in the discovery process which involved a single child as well as in one in which he engages in play activities with others. Children at play spontaneously create a game and then structure it by devising rules. They exalt the humblest play activity by bestowing rules upon it, thus dignifying play sometimes to the point of ritual. The child's simple approach to learning through play is thus characterized as a free and spontaneous activity, yet at the same time as one dependent upon very important rules. To break a rule is to spoil the game. It means starting over again with even more regard for rules. This attention to rules is soon balanced by the spontaneous decision to change the rules or even to begin a new game. The integration of freedom with structure and of creativity with rules achieved by the child learner in simple play is often in contrast to the approach of the adult who tends to devise unnatural methods in his often complex approach to learning.

Throughout this process the child exercises responsibility along with freedom. He freely selects his own course of play and is responsible for his choice. He is responsible to himself for following through on his decision, as long as that decision has meaning and is therefore a means of growth. He is responsible to other players who depend upon his participation in order that the game may be a structured whole within which each player shares. Finally, he is responsible to the rules which are an essential part of play and without which the purpose could not be achieved, the purpose being simply delight in an experience of growth. Only through responsibility to the structural requirements of the growth process can growth occur.

For the pre-school child who has been surrounded by the usual household objects as well as his own toys, which for him are tools of learning, and who in his simple play exercises the delicate balance of freedom with its inherent responsibility, the library-centered approach to learning is natural; it is in accord with his nature and with the way he has always learned. When he enters the primary school and is surrounded there by the tools of a library-media center, he experiences an extension of what his learning environment has always been. He continues to learn through the process of personal discovery within his environment.

For the child learner who has always freely chosen his play things, the process of freely choosing his tools of learning from within the library media center is an extension of his previous experiencing. Also, the child who has learned during five or more years of pre—school play that he is responsible for his choices, continues to grow in responsibility as he is continually trusted to learn how to learn. Finally, the child who has been free to learn independently during the first five years of his life is able to continue to learn in his own way and at his own pace.

The primary school child continues to make discoveries assisted by a facilitator as needed. This too is a continuation of his previous experiencing. As a pre-school child his learning facilitators were likely to have been his parents. These adults provided the tools of learning, such as the play things, and assisted the child in the manipulation and understanding of them. In these ways they guided the child in the process of discovery, a learning approach which will be a part of him throughout life. The child assisted by parent-facilitators at home readily accepts the facilitator at school as someone eho wants him to learn, who encourages him in this process, who shares the delights of learning with him, and who thus promotes the process of growth. The learning facilitator at school is primarily responsible for creating an atmosphere and an environment in which the child can continue his growth process.

It is not only natural that the child learner continue to learn as he has, but it is even necessary that he do so. It is necessary that he exercise his freedom to learn according to the requirements of his nature in order that he not be thwarted in his growth process. It is necessary that the school respect him and his learning process and that it does not inhibit his growth. Such inhibitions may include teacher's lesson plans and other imposed methods of shaping naturally creative individuals into a pre-determined and set mold.

Further, the child learns to be free and to make responsible choices only through experience. Therefore, he needs opportunities for experience. He will not be able to assume responsibility for his education as a junior high school student and certainly not as a college student unless he has learned from earliest years to trust his human nature to make choices. The development of this decision-making ability and the sense of responsibility for these decisions takes place over a period of time and must be begun early in life. As a pre-school child the young learner begins to develop his decision-making ability; he continues this process at school where he grows in becoming an intelligent user of library learning resources.

The child in the primary school has an active curiosity and wants to discover resources which will satisfy his need to know; therefore, he is ideally ready for the learning process which is library and media centered. The young child is, for example, eager to select a library book and to choose from among the other media an item which attracts him. Just as in his pre-school years the child has been free to choose the toy from which he would learn, so in the school library he is free to select learning materials which have meaning for him.

In the case of book selection, the child may choose a particular title for any number of reasons. He may choose a book for its appealing format, colorful illustrations, or satisfying story. He may choose it because he has enjoyed previous experiences with it. The child may choose a familiar old favorite because of the pleasant memories of it, or he may choose a book familiar to him because he needs the security of it. A particular book may be familiar to a child because the story has been read to him, perhaps often. The child may even have read a particular book by himself and continue to want to use it. Therefore, he may repeatedly select it from the library. On the other hand a child may choose a book for its newness quality; he may want something different from any past experience. Whatever the child's reason for selecting a book, both the selection process and the book are meaningful to him. They are meaningful because they represent his needs and interests. A child may even give meaning to a book simply because it is his personal choice.

That a child has his own needs and interests and experiences meaning in his book selection is illustrated in the case of the first grade child, who, within a few weeks of the beginning of the school term, went to the library and asked the librarian for a horse story. The librarian located a book which contained a story about horses, showed the book's illustrations to the child and asked, "Is this the kind of story you'd like?" To which the child replied, "No, it has to be one where the horse goes into water!"

Since this child was as yet unable to read, it is likely that some one had read a horse story to him, and that he enjoyed it so much as to want to hear it again; or perhaps as a beginner in the new experience of school, he needed some assurance and looked for it from a familiar story. Whatever the child's motivation may have been, his readiness for decision-making in his learning process was evident. He knew what he wanted; he was free to choose and reject from among the tools of learning, in this case books; and after having found the story which he had in mind, he felt a responsibility for his choice because it was his personal choice.

A first or second grade child will often go to the library, tell the librarian part of the plot of a story (as much as he recalls), and expect her to find the book for him. This child knows his interests and knows where and how to satisfy them. By pursuing his interests and following wherever they may lead, he is already, in the most simple way, learning how to learn and assuming responsibility for his education. He is forming behavior patterns and making discoveries in a library-media center, independently of other children's needs, and with the assistance of a learning facilitator. Most important of all, he enjoys learning and enjoys books and other resources which are the tools of learning.

Only when his motivation is internal, not imposed, if such be possible, can he experience any permanent change within him. Without such interest and motivation he may remember facts for a time, but he will not acquire understandings, and even the facts will not become a permanent part of him. Without a positive attitude acquired through pleasurable experience, the child may not learn to read at all.

The child forms a positive attitude when his needs and interests are met and when he is in a non-threatening, fear-free atmosphere. The child who is afraid cannot learn. Fear of failure or of displeasing an adult, such as a teacher, preclude the child's possibility of open to receive such openness is an essential requirement of learning. Fear flows from insecurity, and the insecure learner can only seek security, he cannot experience the freedom of learning how to learn.

The child in the primary school is ready for the interdisciplinary approach of library-centered learning. Indeed, all of his pre-school learning has been interdisciplinary. The young child's learning has been interdisciplinary because of his exposure to a wide variety of experiences and because of his natural ability to integrate. He has always seen his world as a whole. His agile mind and active imagination move readily from observation of the activities of an ant hill to listening to a story of fantasy. In either case his learning is problem-centered, not course or discipline-centered. He is not concerned that some of his exposures and experiences may be classified as scientific while others may be labeled appreciation of literature. Rather, the child's energies are concentrated on the reality of the now with its specific problem situation.

The scheme of dividing and classifying knowledge is imposed on the learner only after he begins his formal education, with the separations of knowledge becoming more distinct as he moves higher up the education ladder. As a consequence of these separations of knowledge, the adult learner, if he is to be integrated, needs to reassemble the fragments of his world and recapture the simplicity of the child's discovery approach. The adult needs to restructure his world and re-center himself within it. Only thus can he again understand the world of knowledge as an interdisciplinary whole.

Interdisciplinary learning is continued in the primary school through the library-centered approach in any number of ways. The following anecdote illustrates the manner in which it occurred at one school. One morning a second grade boy returned to the library a book which he had borrowed a few days earlier. The book was about reptiles, and its colorful cover attracted the attention of several other children who were visiting in the library. Together they examined the book, particularly its pictures of unusual reptiles of the past as well as the museums where their likenesses are kept. The children shared with one another what each already knew about reptiles, museums, parks, zoos, or strange animals. Some had seen television programs on these or related topics.

This "discussion" by a group of second graders sparked the interest of one member of the group to pursue his special interest independently. This child read everything in the library, beginning with non-fiction, then moving on to stories of snakes and other pets. He even read encyclopedia and magazine articles. His study of snakes led him to an interest in geographical areas where snakes are found, including deserts and jungles. From here his interests led him to books and other learning resources about various climates and the weather. This opened him to discover biography of explorers of little known polar regions, of airplane pilots who had flown over such regions, on to a study of the mechanics of airplanes themselves. From here the child learner followed the muses wherever 'they led, and thus continued his search for knowledge and understandings, a search which is endless. Through this interdisciplinary approach the child continues to integrate for himself and to see the world of learning as a whole.

In this discovery process the child learner is free to explore among the entire variety and range of library-media center materials. He reads the printed word; he views films and filmstrips; he listens to tapes and records, and he examines pictures, an important way of learning for the child. He uses creative learning tools to build an igloo, to draw a snake, to construct a toy airplane, to design a reptile cage or museum, or to express himself and his discoveries in any other way.

The range of materials include those easily comprehended by

him as well as others which challenge his comprehension. Because he is able to find materials which satisfy his needs, he is not frustrated. Because he is challenged by his interests, free to pursue them, and assured of success, he will accept the challenge of further growth.

Through the library-centered approach the child experiences personal and social responsibility. He shares learning resources with others and realizes his responsibility for the proper care of these materials for the sake of others. Given the freedom to explore among the learning resources of the library, as well as the responsibility for their proper use, the young child understands that these things do not belong to any one person, but are to be used by all. To help the child realize this, the facilitator, especially the librarian, is not possessive about the learning materials, but creates an atmosphere in which the child feels free to exercise his right to use these materials.

Children commonly assume that the school belongs to adults and may be surprised to learn otherwise. This is evident in the following incident. A second grade child approached the librarian and asked, "Has you got THE HAPPY LION?" Not knowing whether or not the library had the book, the librarian said, "I don't know. I'll have to look it up." Taken by surprise the child said, "Don't You know? You own the whole library, don't you?" To this the librarian replied, "No, I don't own these books. I just work here." With that, another child poked the ribs of the first saying, "Dummy, don't you know? The principal owns the whole school!"

In addition to experiencing responsibility for the materials of the learning center, the child also takes his turn at using the facilitator's time. He learns that the facilitator's time belongs to all of the children and that he may not be too demanding of it. He grows in his ability to be independent of the facilitator's assistance and in his ability to learn how to learn in his own way. He learns to learn through social interaction with the facilitator but exercises the restraint required by the society of learners.

The child learner also experiences social interaction with other children. His natural interest in other children leads him to an interest in what they are doing and in what they are learning. He learns to respect the uniqueness of other children, and realizes that he is distinct from them with a right to his own distinctness. Yet from the atmosphere of respect and sharing he learns an interdependence among all of the learners and with the facilitator. Through this approach to learning the child realizes the socialization process.

The primary school child is not only ready for an interdisciplinary approach, but he is also ready to discover the library skills needed to use resources. He can learn the skill required to use the card catalog intelligently. Just as in the case of the older student, the primary child learns this skill within the context of his own need, not as something imposed by a teacher. The child pursuing the study of snakes for example, can discover the subject for snakes or reptiles, or cross references for either, as the case may be.

A divided catalog, at least with the subject cards separate, has advantages for this use, since it simplifies the procedure for finding a particular subject. Learners on this age level are most likely to ask for a book by subject, although they may sometimes remember a particular title and ask for it. Rarely do they ask for a book by author. Therefore, a divided catalog has the advantage of separating the most frequently used cards from those seldom used.

Having found the catalog cards for snakes, the child learns to interpret the classification symbol, since it is simplified for his use. Finally, he learns to locate the snake books on the shelves because all of the shelves are well labeled, perhaps with pictures as well as with words and numbers.

The child who is motivated by his own needs and interests to pursue a particular topic will have the patience and the determination to continue his search and to make a discovery. His drive to have his need fulfilled will sustain him in the learning process, and the effects of that process will be permanent because of his motivation.

The primary grade child who sees a relationship between the card catalog and location of books on the shelves is already well on the way to mastering learning tools. And the child who is free to use these tools and experiment with them, who feels comfortable and at ease in the library, approaches the world of learning with an openness, an eagerness, a readiness not possible to the young child imprisoned in a school where things are more important than people, and where order is preferred to creativity, which is of its very essence haphazard.

The young learner is able not only to choose his own books, but he also can check them out and file his own circulation cards. As soon as the child learns the alphabet, he can learn also to recognize the place of the author's name on the circulation card and he can file these cards behind the appropriate alphabetical index file card. With this approach, the librarian will set up some system of limiting the number of cards in one file, as for example, by having a separate circulation file for a group of children, or through whatever method she considers best.

This child can also stamp his own books and cards with the date due. This may be done by each child independently, or several children may take turns stamping the books for all, and even filing the cards for all. These responsibilities are very important to young learners. They take seriously their role as "stamper" or "filer". Also doing these jobs gives them a sense of responsibility for the library, which they understand as theirs to use, not as the property of the librarian.

There may be any number of other ways in which the child can assist with the proper functioning of the library. In any given situation the ingenuity of the facilitator, teacher or librarian, can match the creativity of the child learner in exploring possible ways of implementing the ideas of library-centered, independent study. The result is a learning environment which serves its purpose of promoting the growth process.

The young learner uses not only printed books but also various items in other media, including the entire range of the generic book. In fact, these items are of particular importance for the young learner who depends largely on seeing, hearing, feeling, and his other senses. All kinds of learning devices are available for this age group and are a part of the learning resources of the library-media center.

The use of the library-media center as described here is based on various assumptions. One assumption is that what matters most is the child's positive experience with the library tools. This experience is acquired day by day as the young learner realizes that the library exists for his needs, that it belongs to him as much as to any one else, and that he is responsible for it. Realizing this, he is comfortable in it; he is not fearful of it; rather, he trusts his ability to master its tools. He experiences the library as a part of all of his learning activities. He identifies learning with living. This positive experience of the child at ease in using the library is more important than that the library be a technically flawless operation.

It is also assumed that the library for primary children be separated from the collection of older students and that it be relatively small. When the library for primary children is a separate facility, it can more readily be exclusively for their use and be their responsibility. A facility which can adequately house several thousand volumes of books, along with a proportionate number of audio-visual items is sufficient and, in fact, far more than any child learner is able to exhaust.

A further assumption basic to this discussion of the library is that the primary grade child can learn to read classification symbols amd can locate needed books. Classification symbols can be simplified so as to be understandable to the child learner and yet be adequate to arrange the materials in the collection. With a relatively small collection this is no problem.

The child learns the use of the library not only in the technical sense of selecting, locating, and checking out books, but also as a place of delight in listening to and reading stories. Indeed, much of the child's motivation for wanting to read and for wanting his own book, comes from the enjoyment which he has experienced in having stories read to him. Therefore, an important function of the primary school librarian is the reading and telling of stories.

Children at this age level are eager to learn and easily remember those things which have meaning for them. They readily latch on to terms of interest to them. Big words are particularly attractive to little people. This is illustrated in the case of the second grade class who has had some experience using the card catalog and other library materials. A librarian preparing to read a new book to them was telling them that on the inside of the front cover of the paper jacket there was a short section describing the story. She said that she would read that to them and then they would decide whether or not they wanted to hear the story. When she had finished, one of the children asked, "Do you mean that's an annotated bibliography?"

This incident is an example of the many unexpected and unpredictable outcomes of a library-centered learning situation, characterized not by rigidity and order, nor by license and chaos, but by the inherent freedom and structural requirements of the situation. Incidents such as this, occurring wherever children are free to learn, illustrate the fact that the creative process, of which learning is a part, cannot be planned. It can only be nourished or repressed. The choice is the responsibility of all persons involved in the education process.

Chapter Seven
Implementing
Library Centered Learning

As indicated in previous chapters, the learning process happens as the individual learner becomes aware of and responds to a personal need to be met. Satisfaction of the need requires that the learner explore a problem, thereby gaining knowledge, understanding, and acceptance of some aspect of life. This chapter will attempt to describe ways in which library centered learning can be implemented to meet a learner's personal need.

One need which the child learner in the primary school experiences is that of expanding his awareness of and relationship with his broadening world. Through library centered learning the child satisfies this need as he communicates with his world through the use of the tools of learning.

These tools include the entire range of the generic book: films, filmstrips, tapes, discs, pictures, pamphlets, charts, books, magazines, newspapers, games, picture and word puzzles, and other objects which communicate to the learner something of his community. The child also learns through field trips to places of interest and through resource persons, such as facilitators.

For the young learner the tools of learning about his local community include books on those occupations represented within the community. Therefore, books on policemen, firemen, bakers, grocers, truck drivers, nurses, sales clerks, teachers, telephone operators, and others are an important means of expanding the learner's view. According to the child's understanding, persons functioning in these occupations may be considered "community helpers."

The child who is motivated to learn about his community chooses to read these books. He selects from among the books of a series on community helpers whatever occupation interests him, or he concentrates on reading all that he can find on one specific occupation. He may, for example, read all that he can on airplane pilots.

In addition to reading from the printed page, the young learner also learns through non-book media. The child has access to the filmstrip collection and filmstrip viewers. With teacher assistance, if needed, the learner selects and views filmstrips on airplane pilots, or on any other occupation represented in the collection and of interest to him. He also views films and listens to recordings relating to his community. Thus, library centered learning requires that he choose his own learning tool and use the tool according to his need.

Because some young learners have a fascination for stories about firemen, the librarian reads on this topic to a group. This initial group experience leads one child to seek out additional books on his own. He learns to use the card catalog and to locate on the shelves books of story and fact about fires, firemen, and fire trucks. He looks up firemen in an encyclopedia and reads the article given there. He gains additional knowledge in the use of the encyclopedia by referring to related articles. He then writes his own story on this topic, using a dictionary and learning new words. In this case the child learner has used basic learning tools: books, encyclopedia, dictionary, and card catalog.

At the same time other children are pursuing their chosen topics in their own ways. Because some children like to have someone listen to them as they read, they may decide to read to one another from among the books they have selected. Thus, the child interested in firemen reads to an audience a story he has discovered. He, in turn, becomes a listener as another child reads about policemen, cowboys, or flight attendants.

As a response to his learning experiences, the child expresses himself and his discoveries in his own unique way. That is, he works out a project. He writes a story about what he learned during a tour of a bakery; he makes a model fire truck; he draws a book of pictures of what he saw on a field trip to the water plant; or he dramatizes the roles of supermarket clerks. Having viewed filmstrips, the child decides to make his own series of pictures about his local community and its people. The child listens to a recording of a song about firemen or railroad engineers or silversmiths, and as a response, he composes his own song about some new discovery relating to his community. Through the use of puppets, possibly of his own creation, the learner re-enacts the story of a zoo keeper. Through pantomime several children express their understanding of the work of a bank teller, or service station attendant, or dentist.

A group of learners decides to create a television program on careers in their community. Having done research through reading books, seeing pictures, or taking field trips, each child contributes an illustration or series of illustrations with a written script accompanying his pictures. The children then combine their efforts. They select announcers, directors, picture-crew, sound-crew, and whoever else is needed for presenting a television program. During this process the children learn about other community helpers, namely, the varieties of personnel required to produce a television program. Important learning occurs as each child learner plans his project and shares his experiences with others.

Throughout this process the teacher and librarian provide learning materials and assist in their use. In the library or media center the librarian arranges an attractive display of the generic book and he places them in the most accessible manner. He gives each learner individual attention as the learner browses and selects a learning tool. The librarian opens to the learner possible uses for a set of slides, for a game or a puzzle, without, however, intruding upon the child's own insight. The teacher, tthoroughly acquainted with library and media-center resources, as well as with the individual learner's needs, unobtrusively assists the learner in communicating with the tools. Teacher and librarian do not show, tell, or lecture the learner on anything which he can discover for himself. The teacher does not dispense any information about these community helpers, rather he assists the learner in his independent search. Both teacher and librarian encourage the child learner to make discoveries; they follow the child's spirit of inquiry wherever it leads, as the child assumes responsibility for learning. The child learner experiences for himself when he is ready. He reads, views, and listens as he needs. This approach provides for interdisciplinary learning as it leads the child into a variety of areas to be explored.

The child in the upper grades of elementary school is curious about many things. His interest in his world extends beyond that of the younger child in the primary grades who is limited to awareness of his local community. The older elementary grade school learner needs to know about people in far-away places. He is interested in persons who live in a country markedly different from his own. Therefore, social studies in the upper elementary grades assumes a broader, global perspective for the learner.

A library centered approach in social studies for the elementary school learner of more advanced years may proceed as follows. The child sees a television program about a foreign country, as for example, Egypt. This motivates him to learn more. He searches everything he can about it in the library and media center. He scans a book on modern Egypt; he studies a filmstrip on the Aswan Dam;

he collects current newspaper and magazine clippings on Egypt, its president, and the Arabs, and compiles them in a scrapbook; he views a film on the Nile; and in the library picture file he finds and studies a series of pictures on ancient Egypt. This latter discovery broadens his approach to his topic so as to include the ancient civilizations of the Middle East. His enthusiasm about his discoveries mounts so that he prepares a slide-tape program on what he has learned, and he shares his discoveries with other students.

Another social studies project develops from a learner's interest in cars: old models, contemporary designs, future trends, racing cars, limousines, etc. The learner who is fascinated with this topic begins by perusing magazine pictures and articles on cars. Gradually he uses the entire range of the generic book: periodicals, books, slides, films, filmstrips, tours of assembly plants, visits with auto dealers, and contact with the actual cars themselves.

In addition to learning about the mechanics and technology of automobiles, the student also learns about the society in which specific cars were used, the kinds of people who used particular kinds of cars, and the persons who were responsible for creating, designing, and manufacturing various models.

While one student pursues this project other students are making discoveries about other forms of land, sea, and air travel, including interplanetary flights. Therefore, some students will learn about man's earliest attempts at flying, the various kinds and use of aircraft, the history of navigation, the story of railroads, and discoveries resulting from space flights. The social implications of the developments of various forms of transportation may be a particular emphasis in each learner's approach. As a result of this way of learning the students will gain an abundance of knowledge and greater understandings of the people and the societies out of which various forms of technology developed.

During this learning process teacher and librarian provide resources and assist the learner in the use of them. The facilitators make available in the library or media center those magazines, books, and other learning tools which the individual learner needs. To insure ready access to these materials the facilitators may sometimes even anticipate learner requests. The facilitators may suggest ways to build a model airplane or a ship or to design a car. They may guide the learner in discovering how to use a periodical index and how to read a road map. They may assist the learner in his understanding of cross references of the card catalog, but never do they interfere with the movements of thinking which the learner experiences.

This approach to learning contrasts with the traditional class-room method in which the teacher meets with twenty-five or more students and instructs through the use of the lecture (telling) and textbooks. It is a procedure in contrast to the traditional approach of teaching individual students as a group, proceeding lesson by lesson, day after day, memorizing whatever information the teacher and the textbook writer think is important.

In contrast with the conventional approach, the library centered approach to learning is without the use of prescribed texts or other teacher selected materials. Instead, with the assistance of facilitators the child learner selects his own books and other resources from the library learning center. He moves about freely choosing books, reading pictures, listening to a talking storybook, viewing a filmstrip, asking questions, observing other learners, thinking, planning, feeling, discovering, evaluating, growing; in short, learning.

The junior high school student has a more specialized interest in his world, and he may expect the social sciences to help him satisfy that interest. For example, he may be interested in knowing about the U.S. Civil War. More specifically, he may be interested in battles of that war. To meet this need to know, the learner reads biography of Civil War generals and other leaders. He reads fiction about the common soldier and the families and places affected by the war. He uses atlases, including historical atlases, to locate places referred to in his reading. He may even compose his own original atlas based on his reading. He uses reference books such as biographical collections and gazetteers, and he reads encyclopedia articles on topics relevant to his search. He uses an index to periodicals to find additional kinds of resources, and he uses a picture file for visual aids. The card catalog refers him to the history section of the library where he finds numerous books on Civil War battles as well as other books which include material pertinent to his search. He learns to use intelligently the tables of contents and indexes of various history books. The learner uses the entire range of the generic book including filmstrips, films, tapes, and other non-print material.

Having discovered an abundance of resource material relating to his interest, the learner selects that which he reads, views, and to which he listens. Because the library centered approach offers a wide range of materials, the learner discovers various, even conflicting, points of view on his chosen topic. Even as a junior high school student he learns to discover differences and to evaluate sources. Thus his opportunities for growth in knowledge and understandings are expanded, his awarenesses broadened, and his insights deepened.

Not only the social sciences but also the natural sciences offer the junior high learner abundant opportunities for discovery. Furthermore, the junior high learner is likely to be interested in numerous areas of science. Beginning with an interest in animals as pets, one learner spends weeks pursuing information and understandings and gaining insights into all areas of animal life: birds, insects, fish, mammals. Through the use of well-illustrated nature magazines the student learns how to care for animal pets, fine points of distinction between different kinds of insects, unusual information about marine biology, and behavlor of migratory birds. His natural curiosity leads him to search all available resources while simultaneously, though unwittingly, he grows in ability to read with increased comprehension.

While one student pursues animal life, another chooses to explore astronomy, and his explorations lead him into problems concerning climate, weather, and eventually physical geography. This kind of exploration leads the learner to various kinds of maps, charts, and globes. He uses atlases, weather charts, and telescopes. As he follows his line of interest, he may delve into study of sun, heat, light, color, energy, or he may turn to deeper interest in the constellations and even mythology.

The culmination of his learning experience may be a time of sharing discoveries among a group of learners. Sharing may take the form of oral presentations; group discussions; original audiovisual programs; written accounts of one's discoveries through essay, poems, dramatic skits, or simple narration; or any other way of expressing oneself and one's discoveries. The wealth of material explored, the richness of personal discovery, and the individual learner's growth through the library-centered learning process are beyond compare with the close of a tranditional unit of study in which the sterility of a final test marks the end of the need to temporarily remember facts.

The function of the teacher throughout this process is to encourage the learner to discover and pursue an interest. The teacher assists in that pursuit by bringing together learner and tools of learning. Teacher and librarian assist the learner in the use of the library including its variety of books, magazines, and other media. In order to do this, both teacher and librarian know subject matter and the bibliographic approaches to it. Following the student's line of inquiry, both teacher and librarian learn ever so much more about science, about people, and about learning, than they ever could in a classroom-textbook approach to a subject.

To the more mature high school student the discipline of the social sciences offers a variety of social problems, many of which have relevance for the young learner and all of which open possibilities for interdisciplinary explorations. The high school learner may decide to puruse the energy problem, which may, in turn, lead him into ecology, economics, politics, government, or some other area.

Because the energy problem is contemporary, the learner begins by searching for current articles on the topic in periodical indexes. He finds there such a large number of articles that he quickly understands that he will be able to read only a very limited amount of material available. At this point the student sees the need to structure his search and to more specifically define his goal. He may decide to read only from among articles in specific periodicals. In deciding from which periodicals to read, he is introduced to sources which evaluate the various periodicals available. In this way the student learns the relative merits of the periodicals and something of their aims and purposes.

In searching the energy crises through periodical indexes, the student learns to master this learning tool. He becomes acquainted with subject headings, subdivisions, and cross references. He learns this tool through use of it in searching a topic which is a problem for him. The learner continues his search through other library learning tools; the library card catalog; almanacs, encyclopedias, and other reference books; file material; as well as non-print media, for which he uses media indexes.

The facilitators, teacher and librarian, provide an environment in which the learner can satisfy his need to know through making his own discoveries. The facilitators provide learning resources and assistance in using them. They alert the learner to possible new avenues of exploration, thus indicating the possibilities for an interdisciplinary approach. The teacher, who is a subject specialist, has knowledge of the range and depth of works throughout the discipline; while the librarian, who is a bibliographic expert, is aware of means of exploring all possible tools of communication. However, both share in the expertise of the other, and together they serve to facilitate the independent study of the learner.

Concurrent with his independent study of the energy problem, the adolescent learner also pursues other subjects. He spends his day reading, writing, viewing, listening, speaking, discussing, thinking, and feeling. He participates in all of these activities as one internally motivated. He consults the facilitator, plans with peers, corresponds with professional persons, discusses with a group, and expresses his thoughts and feelings through writing and other creative processes. He learns to know himself and others. He learns to relate with others. He becomes aware of the world outside of the school. He learns to find and use learning resources, materials as well as persons. Through these experiences he develops intellectually, personally, and socially. He creates himself in this process of learning how to learn.

In library-centered learning, these activities are not structured so as to occur during specific hours and in particular rooms. Rather, the learner fits these activities into the structural whole of his learning situation. Therefore, the adolescent studying the energy problem reports to a group and discusses with others, not on a topic or at a time decided by another, but when he needs to share something which he has discovered and which has meaning for him.

The learner in the college brings to the study of the social sciences a broad world view and wide ranging interests. He is aware of current issues and contemporary problems which he sees as relative to himself and his local community as well as to the larger global community. Therefore, the library centered and independent study approach on the college level happens as the learner pursues his interest in still another social science area, as for example, U.S. foreign policy. As did the younger student, so too the college student quickly sees the need to define his search, if for no other reason than the vast amount of material available.

The learner procedes in his search through bibliographies and indexes, through newspapers, magazines, books, and non-print media; through standard reference sources, card cataloges, and pamphlets. In addition to using a general periodical index, the college learner also uses specialized subject indexes. This bibliographic approach provides limitless opportunities for further pursuits.

Throughout this process the learner discovers various points of view on his chosen topic; he learns the editorial policies, or biases, of the journals used; he becomes aware of the wide range of material available on the topic, of the variety of approaches to it, of the numerous tools from which to choose. Most importantly, he grows in awareness of the interdisciplinary nature of knowledge.

For the high school or college student, social studies or an understanding of one's world may begin with the front page, editorial page, or in fact, any page of the daily newspaper. Articles there lead the learner to research the use of any one of the natural resources, U.S. relationship with another country, taxation in American life, the First Amendment, the psychology of violence, the role of corporations, fiscal management, or any number of problems affecting society. Researching such a problem will involve the student with the use of periodical indexes, almanacs, encyclopedias, journals, documentaries, statistics, indeed, with the entire range of the generic book.

The learner could compare newspapers, one with another as to ways in which news is handled. The printed word could be compared with the spoken word of radio or television. Daily papers could be compared with weeklies or even with news magazines and journals. A student may decide to follow one particular kind of news story through all or several of these ways. Such a method not only sharpens the reader's critical powers, but also keeps him informed of happenings. The student could use other library resources, such as scholarly books and journals, for background information or researched opinions on the topic of his choice.

The instructor guides the learner to the available resources and facilitates their use. In order to know what library and media center can offer, the instructor is a bibliographic expert. He has knowledge of the various indexes, guides, catalogs, and other bibliographies; and he assists the learner in evaluating and choosing from among these tools. The librarian who facilitates this learning approach is not only a bibliographic expert, but is also a subject specialist so that he too can intelligently assist the learner with his search.

Regardless of whether the learner is entering the primary school, secondary school, or college, the facilitator and he jointly plan a line of action. The facilitator encourages the learner to discover his emergent need or interest which serves as a springboard for learning. As one who prompts the learner to motivate himself, the facilitator is responsible for helping the learner become conscious of his needs, desires, and interests. The facilitator creates situations which prompt the learner to receive insights by which to perceive his needs. The facilitator understands human nature and recognizes the learner's need to discover and explore his world. Therefore, the facilitator prompts the learner to educate himself, to create himself, and to increase in consciousness through interaction and interrelationship with his world.

The basic means for interacting, for relating, for discovering and exploring, as well as the basic need and desire of every learner, whether he is conscious of it or not, is reading. Thus, the facilitator assists the learner in the process of discovering his need to read and of realizing this ability. The child learner spends much of his time experiencing reading, and, as indicated previously, to be a true experience, the reading process is organic. The adolescent and young adult learner also read, using the entire range of the generic book in an exploration of an emergent interest.

In order to implement a library centered approach to learning one replaces the artificial structures of rigid schedules, definite class periods, and specific courses, credits, and grades, with the structural requirements of the learning situation. These structural requirements, based on the nature of the learner, provide him with the conditions needed to complete gestalts in his learning experiences. Thus, for example, the adolescent learner searching the energy problem spends as much time as he needs in reading about it. He is not quizzed at the end of every chapter or once a week, or within any other artificial structure. Rather he is permitted to study independently, to question, to explore, and so to fulfill his emergent interest. Having completed the study of this topic according to his satisfaction, he experiences a gestalt. He does not memorize information, but is provided the opportunity to learn what he needs and in the best way for him.

Without the traditional, although artificial structures which dominate and determine so much in schools and colleges, will the learner become competent in reading, writing, arithmetic? A positive response to the above query is that the student will become competent in reading, writing, arithmetic, only if he desires it, is internally motivated, and has the opportunity to learn according to the needs of his nature. On the other hand, one may not simply assume that traditional schooling has produced competent readers, writers, and mathematicians; whereas, in fact, the failures of the traditional system are too gross to be overlooked and too glaring to be concealed. Not only has the traditional educational system failed to produce subject specialists; worse, it has failed to send forth from schools and colleges personally mature and whole individuals, capable of meeting the challenge to live fully.

What does education mean to the teen-ager who seems to have no interest in anything relating to school, who does not know how to profit from time and experience, who is directionless, who couldn't care less? Has such a one ever been permanently helped because of the traditional school system? Rather, has it not more often embittered and turned-off a young person who could learn, but not according to the what, when, how, and where of an authority figure? How many legions of drop-outs could have been prevented through a more flexible, humane, human approach to learner needs?

What concern has traditional education for the adolescent who "puts in time" in school, bored, disgusted, frustrated, because he is not able to learn according to the system and because his unique needs are not even considered? Why must the one same curriculum be served to all? Why, for example, must everyone spend the same number of years, studying history, mathematics, language arts, and science?

What grade or high school principal has ever walked through the halls of his school and not heard teachers dispense information which he himself did not know? And if successful adults do not need to have memorized the skeletal system of the frog, the chief export of England; and the square root of eight, then why inflict young learners with such facts? Many of the facts "learned" one year will have changed before the learner completes his formal education, but the process of learning remains with the learner forever.

Certainly teen-agers will learn subject matter, but it will be as an outcome of the process of self-directed learning, not as an end in itself. Immersed in the literature of numerous subjects, the learner in the library grows through contact and involvement with resources and the tools of learning. He grows because his nature pre-disposes him to growth, growth in every way, intellectual, sensitive, intuitive, and insightful. All of these learnings are his in a learning environment which respects the learner's nature.

One may ask how a library-centered approach to learning would meet and satisfy state and accrediting agency requirements, perhaps especially in relation to curriculum, numbers of courses offered or taken, hours, credits, and grades given or received. In response, one may question the validity of existing requirements. Is not the reason for any school or college that of providing whole persons, citizens knowledgeable and wise, who can continue active participation in a free society? If this is so, then of what significance is the mere fact that one has put in sufficient time to acquire thirty credits in world history, or that one has covered the entire text in fourth grade science? Perhaps requirements should be stated in terms of intellectual, personal, and social maturity, rather than of courses offered, credits and grades acquired. Would not a file of written descriptions of specific competencies acquired be more meaningful?

Of what value are traditional requirements when proofs of failure of the system are so obvious? What teacher has ever known a group of students whose capabilities were in accord with the achievement indicated on his record? What teacher in grade six has not known a reading range of six years among students in his class, according to a standardized test? Why is a student in fourth grade unable to do second grade math? Why, therefore, is he in fourth grade? Why do college teachers complain that juniors majoring in science cannot write a complete paragraph?

While subject matter: history, science, math, and language is important in the learning process, does a rigid approach to them through numbers of hours, courses, and grades necessarily assure society that the learner will become equipped through systematic exposure? Does having had three years of high school social studies assure society of better citizens?

Rather, because these subjects are important, the approach must be flexible. If anything is important to all learners, it must accommodate itself to all. If important, it must of its nature be flexible to meet the needs of unique learners.

The library-centered approach to learning in school or college as described here bears some similiarity to learning through the local public library. Both approaches afford the learner free access to the materials of learning and both provide assistance as needed. The outcomes of learning in these situations also are similar. The outcome of learning according to the public library approach is the proverbial little old man, who, having pursued his interests in the midst of interdisciplinary resources, emerges with ever new and broadening knowledge and wisdom as one who continually creates himself through his independent approach to learning. The outcome of learning in the library centered school or college is the young learner progressing in the direction of wholeness.

Chapter Eight
The Wholeness of a Library-Centered Approach to Learning

A library-centered approach to learning provides wholeness in the learning process. This wholeness means that all elements necessary for the process are included and respected. These elements are all persons, materials, and actions involved in the learning process. The persons involved are the learners and the facilitators. Wholeness learning respects the nature of these persons and is based primarily upon the reality of the relationship which exists among them.

In a wholeness approach to learning there is a real relationship between all of the component factors, not only between the persons. Rather, all of the elements which constitute the process are necessarily interconnected. Persons, materials, and actions interact and interrelate. Further, the relationship between these elements is not interrupted anywhere. Therefore, the learning process is one continuous whole. Because it is one continuous whole, no part of the learning process may be lacking.

In wholeness learning all of the components of the process are meaningful in their interrelationships. That is, all of the persons, the material resources, and the actions relate in a meaningful way among themselves. These elements which constitute wholeness learning are related to one another in an integral way; they are not merely accidental or random as are the distinct parts of an aggregate Because whole does not mean all, only those components of the learning process which interrelate meaningfully can really belong in the process.

A learning process characterized by wholeness constitutes a totality which has a structure. This structure of the components as they must be related in view of the learning process encompasses the entire process. Within the learning situation the structure provides the learner with the opportunity to experience wholeness throughout his process of self-creation.

The wholeness approach to learning integrates the roles of the facilitators within the school setting. The facilitators are all of those persons needed in order that the learner may create himself. These persons include the teachers and librarians, all of whom share with the learner and with the other facilitators whatever of himself, his experience, or his ideas may be called forth by a particular situation. The roles of the facilitators may include advising the learner as to a course to pursue, guiding him in the literature of a subject, assisting him in the use of learning tools, stimulating the learner's interest in divergent areas, being for the learner an exemplar of scholarship, leading him to the delights and joys of exploration and discovery, and encouraging him by helping him understand that all of his efforts can be meaningful and can lead to growth. All of these functions are proper to teachers and librarians since this wholeness approach unifies the functions of all persons who assist the learner in whatever way in the education process.

The functions of the facilitators are unified so as to constitute an organism, since the very act of facilitation is a living, growing, changing thing. The processes of advising, guiding, stimulating, being, and encouraging are all life-giving processes; and the interaction of individuals with one another in these ways is a living and life-giving process. Therefore, whatever role the facilitators assume for the moment, it is a vital element in the learning experiences of the learner.

The facilitators, whether librarians or teachers, work with a singleness of purpose. This means that all have in mind and in heart the one same goal and work in harmony in method to achieve that goal. The goal toward which all efforts are directed is that of contributing to the growth process of learning. The facilitators cooperate with each other and function as a unified whole in this common endeavor. Viewed in this way, the roles of the facilitators ultimately become just one role, namely, that of providing a setting in which creation can flourish. Whatever talents one brings to the education process are therefore directed toward the work of releasing creative energies inherent within the learners and facilitators.

Wholeness learning integrates the various disciplines or branches of knowledge so that all branches are seen as a part of a unified whole. Learning which is centered within the library happens within the context of resources representing many disciplines as well as various guides to them, thus promoting opportunities for understanding interrelationships. The disciplines are seen to be interrelated as the learner experiences a method of learning which uses various disciplines and a variety of media and which is for life.

The learner approaches all disciplines through the art of reading, which is a process of understanding the significance of anything as its message reaches the learner through any of his senses. Reading, whether of words, numerals, or other symbols is seen as the basic skill and unifying element. All of learning is basically a learning how to read. In this connection, the statement of Thomas Carlyle holds true. "If we think of it, all that a university, or final highest school can do for us, is still but what the first school began doing, — teach us to READ."[1]

The learner who is free to discover the structure of knowledge, that is, its connectedness, and who experiments with the process of deriving one idea from another, is himself in process of evolution. The process of learning to view all disciplines as an integrated whole promotes the student's growth toward an integrated individual. The integrated learner unifies, makes one within himself, his person and his experiences. As he does so his sense of self-identity is strengthened. The learner perceives the relationship between himself as a person and as a learner. This approach to learning gives the student a sense of the power of his mind and therefore assures him of success in mastering the material world. Thinking which is free to discover relationships rather than being limited within disciplines forms the basis for intelligent thought and prepares the learner for meeting life as a whole. When learning is individualized, all avenues through all disciplines are open to exploration. As the learner chooses his own path, wherever it may take him, all experiences are interrelated and his search is continuous.

Wholeness learning relates the learner with his unique ways of learning. That is so because learning is seen as an activity flowing from the learner, his needs, values, and motivations. Since the learner has his own reason for his behavior, and learning is one aspect of his behavior, his learning method or style is as unique as his personality. The way he learns is consistent with who he is, what he needs, what he values, and how he behaves. That is, the learner's way of learning is consistent with his identity as a person. Given the freedom to learn in a manner consistent with his being, the learner is likely to generalize what he has learned into a style of inquiry that serves for almost any kind of task. He begins to contrast his own process of organizing what he has learned and makes transference as needed.

The process of learning which realizes permanent growth is a process in internalization. The learner digests, assimilates, and is formed by whatever he experiences from a learning situation and by the way in which he experiences. Conversely, the depth, intensity and breadth of his experiencing are based upon what he, as an individual, brings to the learning process.

Library-centered learning relates all possible places of learning both within and outside of the school setting. Such a relationship is possible because a wholeness approach to learning recognizes that the learner's entire range of experiences, whether in school or out of school, can be means through which he increases his consciousness. Relating all possible places of learning removes conflicts in the learner's mind which may prevent his seeing knowledge and his world as a unified whole. With such conflicts removed, the learner makes relationships between in-school and out-of-school experiences and sees both kinds as supplementing and complementing the other.

The school setting which is library-centered can be for the learner a microcosm where he may explore, at least vicariously, any facet of the world which he encounters outside of the school. Understood in this way, the library, with its resource persons and materials, may be seen as a slice of life. The library is a special resource center which provides the tools needed for encountering the world.

Wholeness learning relates the act of learning with the whole of life. The act of learning is an experience of insight. It is a perception into the meaning and relationship of things. Such experiences form a part of every learner's life. With each new insight comes increased consciousness which, in turn, makes possible further insights. Viewed in this way, the act of learning is understood as an exercise of the highest human powers, as life lived at greatest intensity, of thinking, deciding, willing, perceiving, and feeling.

Insight gives consciousness of structural inner relatedness, so that the learner who experiences an insight sees a wholeness about reality. A learning situation which builds on the wholeness of the learner, of the act of learning, and of reality promotes awareness of the unity between life and learning. Such a learning situation also assists the learner to apply what is recalled of insights, not blindly, but in accordance with the structural requirements of the situation. Therefore, wholeness learning assists the learner in perceiving relationships between the act of learning and the whole of life.

This wholeness approach to learning further relates the act of learning with the whole of life by helping the learner develop attitudes of looking for objective structural requirements of a situation, of feeling its needs, not proceeding willfully but as the situation demands. With such an attitude the learner faces issues openly and freely and proceeds to meet them with confidence and courage.

Following the wholeness approach to learning, the learner understands that the functional meaning, that is, the meaning which changes as thinking advances, is of utmost importance. Without it, thinking gets sterile. Without realization of that change, one does not grasp the line of progress. Being vulnerable to these changes, the learner forgets about himself in the process of thinking. He is therefore open to receive insights and perceive structures.

Wholeness learning relates the learner as creature with the rest of creation. The library-centered wholeness approach situates the learner in such a way that he sees himself as part of the on-going process of cosmic creation. He sees himself in relationship with the rest of the world. He realizes that he cannot depend upon himself for his existence, but that he shares the universe with and is in various ways dependent upon other people, other life, and his total environment. Because he is related to, dependent upon, and an integral part of the world, the learner realizes also his responsibility for creation, especially for the creation of other people.

In a wholeness approach to learning, the library setting provides the learner with opportunity to live experiences of relation. The learner relates for himself the multi-media tools of learning with his own senses and learns how each sense assimilates something of the message from the media. The learner relates the uses of these media since they supplement and complement other media in wholeness learning; and he relates uses to which information thus gained may be put. The learner also relates the ways in which resource persons may assist him, persons such as librarians, teachers and peers. In these ways he relates himself to his surroundings as he grows in the process of becoming a part of the world and a participator in his and its creation.

Because it emphasizes life as a process, the wholeness approach to learning helps the learner to develop an historical perspective, that is, to see himself as a link in a chain of evolution and as dated. Therefore, he respects what has gone before and builds on the living tradition of the present. He sees his place in time and in history and is conscious of the open-ended reality of his situation. Such a learner possesses a joy in his ability to share in an undertaking, in a reality, more enduring than himself.

The function of the library in wholeness learning is to provide the learner with opportunities to live out experiences of integration, which is a process of bringing together the parts to form an harmonious whole and which results from organic learning. Teaching situations. Such integration is accomplished through the processes of centering, structuring, and discovering.

Centering refers to the way the learner views the parts which constitute the learning situation in relation to his potential of the present moment. These parts include: himself as learner, his personalized way of learning, his needs and motivations, resource persons, and tools of learning in various media formats. The learner views these parts from his perspective based on past experiences and the possibilities of the present learning environment. He sees all aspects of the learning process as centering on his present creative potential.

Centering refers also to the meaning and roles of the parts as determined in their relation to the entire learning process. Since the meaning and roles are parts of an organic process, they change as the learning situation progresses. Although the parts of a learning situation change, so long as they are seen in relation to the whole, they contribute to the process of integration.

Structuring refers to a regrouping with regard to the whole, a reorganization and a fitting of parts together. In this process the factors of inner relatedness and inner requirements are discovered, realized, and followed up. These operations are done in view of the whole situation. The content, direction, and application grow out of the requirements of the problem. All operations arise because of their part-functions in arriving at a solution. All operations are viewed and treated in regard to their structural place, role, and dynamic meaning, including the realization of the changes which this involves. Realizing structural transposability, structural hierarchy, and separating structurally peripheral from fundamental features, which is a special case of grouping, the learner searches for structural rather than piecemeal truth.

The library provides the learner with opportunity for structuring. Surrounded by the tools of learning in their various formats, by inexhaustive subject matter resources, and by a comprehensive supply of various kinds of media, the learner is ideally situated to regroup, to reorganize, to fit parts together. Situated in the midst of the sum total of man's communication possibilities and not being limited to a particular discipline or method, he views the world to be learned from the broadest perspective possible. He is thus able to discover inner relatedness and the inner requirements of a situation. For him the process of learning happens in view of one whole situation. All tools, disciplines, and media are considered in their structural role and dynamic meaning.

Integration is accomplished not only through centering and structuring, but also through the process of discovery. Discovery is a matter of envisaging, going deeper into questions in order to arrive at a new insight, which, in fact, may not be a solution to a problem, but an experience from which a certain new question may arise. The learner who is situated in the midst of learning resources and who handles directly the tools of learning is free to pursue knowledge and understandings, proceeding in whatever direction his spirit leads him, thus making possible his own personal discoveries. Through these discoveries, which have personal meaning for him, the learner achieves further integration.

Because the library-centered approach to learning is a wholeness approach, it provides the learner with the opportunity to discover gestalts, thus enabling him to see and understand basic patterns and relationships as he encounters the world of persons and stuff in his personal learning process. These patterns and relationships cannot be reduced to simple components, since the structural whole of anything is greater than the sum of its parts. For example, the wholeness of the world of knowledge is greater than the sum of the separate disciplines. Also the wholeness of the organic functions of facilitators is greater than the sum of the distinct roles assumed by all of them.

Also, the learner sees his own learning process, or the act of creation happening within him, against the background of his life as a whole. He perceives the act of learning as part of and relational to his whole life, yet the latter not being as clearly defined as the former. The learner, therefore, sees the wholeness of life and learning and is aware of a pattern being accomplished through his life experiences. He also sees a structure in the ways of learning. He realizes that beyond all of the separate elements which constitute the learning process is a unifying structure which gives meaning to a wholeness which is greater than the sum of its parts.

The learner is able to understand such a wholeness through insight. Insight may be described as the sudden perception of relationships that lead to the solution of a problem. Insight results through the restructuring of thinking or renewal of mind. That is, insight happens as the learner reorganizes what is already there, searches for new relationships, or brings in new possibilities This process helps the learner perceive the situation in a different light so that the solution abruptly suggests itself. The basic idea is one of organization and reorganization.

Since library-centered learning is a wholeness approach, it can help the student transfer insight from one situation to another, thereby assisting him in the process of continually reorganizing his thinking and perceiving meaningful relationships in unlimited situations. For the learner this is not a process that moves from pieces to an aggregate, from below to above, but from above to below, from the nature of the structural problem to the concrete steps toward understanding.

A learning process which provides opportunity for self-creation thereby assists the learner in his coming to know himself. This same process provides for the development of the fully functioning person who, because of his self-knowledge, integrates within himself his potential with his goals and his real self with his ideals. Such integration can take place only when there is great simplicity. Only the integrated person possesses the knowledge of self and therefore the freedom from affectedness which simplicity requires.

The learner who possesses these qualities knows and accepts himself and can integrate his realness at any given moment with the open-ended possibilities provided by life's experiences. Such a learner has a realistic confidence in the use of his thought and of his other powers. He also has images of excellence which he is able to translate into realistic terms for himself.

The wholeness approach of library-centered learning assists the learner to discover for himself those techniques by which he responds to the creative impulse. The techniques are consistent with the being of the learner and arise from the creative impulse itself. Through his response to a creative impulse, he learns his own technique and further integrates his real self with his knowledge of who he is.

The process of integrating within himself includes responding to truth as he hears it and acting upon it by taking it into himself. Failure to so act upon a truth results in its becoming a poison within which brings about an imbalance. As Thomas Carlyle has said, "The new truth, new deeper revealing of the secret of this universe, is verily of the nature of a message from on high; and must and will have itself obeyed."[2]

The learner who has experienced the library-centered approach to wholeness relates to the world as a participator. He realizes prolongations of his own being throughout the world and is astonished at the extent and intimacy of his relationship with the universe. Such a learner understands that there is nothing in man which was not first in the ameba. The learner who relates to his world sees the whole history of the world in part reflected in him and understands that he is forever incorporated into successive influences. The learner sees himself as inseparable from the universe as he realizes that his senses and insights order and assimilate the flow of cosmic influences which merge into his life. Such a learner understands that the totality of the energies of the earth affect him, thus establishing an intimate and permanent relationship between the learner and his universe. This relationship between the learner and an unfolding universe has been expressed thus: ". . . You are a child of the universe, no less than the trees & the stars; you have a right to be here. And whether or not it is clear to you, no doubt the universe is unfolding as it should."[3]

Library-centered wholeness learning results in increased unity of mankind. This approach to learning assists each learner in the process of self-creation, which is a process of developing greater being, and as each learner realizes his own being, so too a unity among all learners results. Because of the interrelatedness among persons and with the universe, a fuller development of any one person or element affects also the entire world and its people. Therefore, as a single learner realizes his potential, he further creates himself and his world by reason of his bonds to it. Thus, in turn, all other learners are affected because they encounter and are encountered by a world of people and stuff which has been changed because of the presence of one learner.

The realization of the interrelatedness and unity of all peoples depends upon the depth of a learner's sensibility and the development of his consciousness. The wholeness approach to learning provides experiences which develop the learner's sensibility and which create conditions for insight to happen. Thus, it is possible for the world to be revealed to the learner and for him to be deeply aware of it.

The learner who has come to see the world as a whole and himself as an integral part of it, also comes to realize his own identity in the context of community. In fact, he learns who he is only in relation to other people and the world of stuff, since all parts of the whole world are interdependent upon one another and have their meaning only in the context of the whole. This interrelatedness among the parts provides a structure for the whole and results in a whole which is greater than the sum of all the parts.

As the learner realizes his identity, he also enjoys greater unity within himself. Greater unity within the individual means that he has acquired greater being, since he has released his creative potential and has more nearly become a complete, perfected person.

Greater fullness of being within a learner is realized as he attains the furthest possible limit of differentiation from all other persons. The more fully he realizes himself, his pecularities, and his own uniqueness, the more he becomes aware of his distinction and difference from others.

The great challenge for each learner is to be united with others, that is, to become the other, while remaining himself. Pestalozzi has described this process of education in these words: "Education is nothing more than the polishing of each single link in the great chain that binds humanity together and gives it unity. The failings of education and human conduct spring as a rule from our disengaging a single link and giving it special treatment as though it were a unit in itself, rather than a part of the chain. It is as though we thought the strength and utility of the link came from its being silver-plated, gilded, or even jeweled, rather than from its being joined unweakened to the links next to it, strong and supple enough to share with them the daily stresses and strains of the chain."[4]

The challenge for everyone involved in the learning process is to grow in the understanding that the release of the creative energies of each person results only insofar as he remains consciously united with his fellowmen and the world. This union with the rest of the world is the context, or chain, from which the single link gets its meaning. The realization of his meaning depends upon a learner's power to contribute to the strength of the chain, that is, to serve as a member of a heterogeneous whole and to harmonize all distinctions within himself.

[1]Thomas Carlyle, *On Heroes, Hero-Worship And The Heroic In History, p. 162.*

[2]Ibid., p. 194.

[3]Desiderata. 1692 (scroll)

[4]Heinrich Pestalozzi, *The Education of Man: Aphorisms, p. 32*

Chapter Nine
Reading:
An Experience of Wholeness

Whether the learner is in the primary school or in a college environment, one activity predominates throughout his process of learning. That is the activity of reading. In this context reading is that activity of the learner in which he concentrates all of his energies upon symbols found in the learning environment and intergrates the meaning of these symbols within himself. These symbols include letters, words, numerals, sounds, pictures, and other sensible representations provided by learning tools. Other kinds of symbols found in the learning environment are the behaviors of learners and facilitators. The learner reads all of these symbols and becomes integrated with them.

Within the learning environment the learner reads the materials of the library; that is, he reads the entire range of the generic book. He reads not only with his eyes, but he concentrates with all of his powers upon the learning tools of his choice. The learner reads the meaning of a film as he watches, listens, and assimilates; he reads a science experiment as he carries it out; and he reads from the pages of a book.

The learner experiences the reading activity sometimes independently from the activities of other learners, sometimes in union with them. Because a library-centered approach to learning provides for independent study, the learner reads as an individual or as a member of a group, silently or aloud. The choice is the learner's, and it depends upon his needs which reading fulfills.

In addition to reading the resources of the library, the learner reads also the learning environment. That is, both consciously and unconsciously, the learner imbibes the atmosphere of the learning environment. The learner feels the freedoms or restraints which are part of the learning situation. He senses the environment and realizes whether he is a participator in a creative process or a prisoner shackled by another's definitions.

The learner reads the learning environment in accord with his previous experience. If previous learning environments have been places of trust, and if his previous experience with the educational process has been a creative growth process, the learner brings to the present learning situation expectations of the same. He reads the learning environment with an attitude of hope. This positive attitude prompts him to search for opportunities for growth.

In addition to reading the environment and the tools within it, the learner reads also the spirit of the facilitator. The learner reads this spirit according to the wholeness which is his. The learner who is becoming whole is open to experience. He listens to himself, others, and the world. Because of this openness, he enjoys a purity of mind and heart which makes possible his discerning the spirit of another, namely, the facilitator. This openness to accept reality is the basis for the learner's objectivity which is required to listen perceptively to another, thus discerning the spirit of another.

The learner who is open to listen and to receive is thus able to read the spirit of the facilitator. He is able to perceive the facilitator's motivation. By concentrating his attention on the behavior of the facilitator, the learner reads and discovers the person of the facilitator. Since this person is pre-eminently significant to the learning process, his need for integrity, for wholeness, for freedom is paramount.

When reading a symbol, including one descriptive of the atmosphere of a place or the spirit of a person, the learner attempts to understand a meaning beyond that of the representation. Just as the letters, words, pictures, or other symbols used in the generic book indicate a meaning beyond themselves, so too the indicators experienced by the learner in his environment point to a meaning which symbols merely attempt to convey. The learner who is open, receptive, and listening, discerns the meaning beyond the symbols. He discerns the trust of human nature which symbols of the learning environment indicate. Such a learner also discerns the freedom, wholeness, and integrity which the behavior of the facilitator symbolizes. The learner perceives the realness of the facilitator. He sees and understands beyond the behavior of the facilitator to the spirit of the person which such behavior represents. The simple, unaffected learner is particularly keen to sense and understand another person.

In a library-centered approach to learning the learner has an opportunity to become whole through the example of the facilitator, who is whole. Through reading the spirit of the facilitator, the learner understands the meaning of wholeness as realized in the life of a person. Recognizing this value, the learner is motivated to discover it within himself. The example of the facilitator proves that wholeness can be realized and that its impact can be felt.

This approach to learning also offers the facilitator the opportunity to be a whole person. It frees him from any constricting role as an authority, a specialist, or an expert who has all of the answers. It frees him to be a creative learner alongside of the student.

As indicated above, the process of reading requires that the learner concentrate upon the symbol being read as a means of understanding the meaning beyond the symbol. The learner concentrates by bringing all of his powers to bear upon the symbol of a reality. As the learner concentrates all of his energies on a particular symbol, an understanding of the reality beyond the symbol comes to the learner as a reward for his labors, as an insight.

Having read the symbol and having received an insight, the learner assimilates the meaning of the symbol. As he assimilates, he becomes one with that reality. The learner's life becomes enriched through his sharing in a reality beyond himself.

The sharing of reality is a process of integration. But integration happens only when there is fidelity to the structural requirements of the situation. These structural requirements include the processes of centering, organizing, and discovering.

In order for integration to occur, the learner first experiences centering. The learner centers himself with the symbol he reads and with the reading process. He experiences himself as relational to the reading activity. By experiencing himself in relation with the symbols he reads and the meaning he assimilates, the learner shares in a reality beyond himself and becomes integrated with it and within himself.

The child reader becomes integrated through the activity of reading a picture. He concentrates on the symbol before him and receives understandings from the picture. He becomes integrated through this process as he experiences himself as relational with it. The child learner relates himself with the learning tool, the picture, and its meaning for him. He experiences himself in relation to his reading and understanding.

Integration also requires that the learner structure his learning situations. That is, he exercises the freedom to regroup the symbols which he reads and from which he receives meaning and insights. He also structures or regroups the meanings and insights derived through them. In this process the learner experiences a personal control over how and what he learns.

The child learner who reads a picture determines the order of his experience. As he sees, reads, and concentrates, he organizes, aesthetically and intellectually. Through the process of organization, the child learner derives meaning from the picture.

Finally, the learner who experiences integration, first experiences the process of discovery, since this process is a structural requirement of the learning situation. The child learner who reads the picture is free to make his own discoveries, and, in fact, needs to discover for himself if he is to become integrated. Only through the process of discovery can the learner personalize his learning so that it has meaning for him. Discoveries have meaning for the learner when these discoveries relate to him. When the learner experiences a personal relationship with his discoveries, he becomes integrated with them. As the child learner reads, he discovers meanings, and he relates these to himself. As with centering and structuring, so in discovering, the learner is an active participator in that creative process through which he is changed.

The learner participates in that process pre-eminently as a reader. As he reads, he centers, structures, and discovers. These activities, in turn, are provided in a learning situation which is characterized as library-centered. In a library-centered approach to learning the learner is free to choose his reading resources from the entire range of the generic book. He is free to choose that which meets his needs. He is free to use the tools of learning as they relate to his needs. Given these freedoms to read, the learner experiences the creative process of integration within him and with his world. The library-centered approach respects and builds on the learner's need for integration, a need fulfilled through the process of reading.

The approach to learning which provides for integration thereby offers the learner the opportunity to experience a gestalt, which is an experience of wholeness. A gestalt experience is one through which the learner grows in his awareness of the wholeness of reality. Through a gestalt experience the learner himself becomes whole. As a whole person, he is a healthy person; he is in harmony with himself and with his world.

A young child experiences a gestalt through such a simple activity as listening to a story being read to him. The gestalt happens as the child not only listens to the words, the symbols, but also as he reads the meaning beyond the words. As he listens and reads, the child experiences himself as relational to the symbols and meanings. He centers himself within the reading process, organizes his sensible and intellectual energies and outcomes, discovers meaning, and integrates his discoveries within himself.

In order that the reading process is a gestalt experience for the child, the story is presented as a whole so that the child can receive it as a whole. Therefore, the story, piece of literature which it is, is not analyzed for the child. The adult who reads the words of the story for the child learner does not attempt to structure or organize the story for the child. He does not attempt to transfer his perceptions and meanings to the child. He does not tell the child what to listen for or suggest meanings. Rather, the teacher trusts that the child can and will use his own energies to center, structure, and discover for himself. The result for the child is therefore a whole and unified experience; whereas, if a teacher were to impose his powers upon the child, the result would be distraction of the child's energies and destruction of his gestalt.

Analysis destroys wholeness. When so much in education from kindergarten through university is broken down into parts: segmented, fractured, divided into disciplines, courses, and even mini-courses; the result for the learner, especially for his mental health, can only be devastating. The learner needs experiences of wholeness. Such experiences can be had through literature, including children's stories, when the teacher resists the temptation to analyze the piece of art. Rather, a facilitator who nourishes learner growth, accepts and trusts the child to feel, intuit, and think for himself. The young learner is capable of accepting a work of art as a whole; in fact, he may be more capable in this way than an adult, since the latter may tend to dissect in order to understand, whereas the child accepts wholeness,

The child who has learned to read words for himself experiences a gestalt in an even more personal way than when someone else reads to him. In the former case the child not only understands meaning and receives insight through symbols he reads, but he learns to savor the symbols for the hidden meanings contained. Reading for himself, the child experiences even greater involvement with the process.

Because he is able to read for himself, the child reads, ponders, and reflects upon the story according to his needs, at his pace, and in accord with his understanding. The child reads the story when he needs and as often as he needs. He exercises control over the story; he uses it as he wills. He centers the story within his life; therefore, he sees himself in relation to it. He structures or regroups the symbols and meaning of the story according to his learning needs. Because he reads, the child makes his own discoveries with the story, perhaps a different discovery each time he reads it.

Not only the young learner, but the learner of any age, so long as he is receptive and reads, can have a gestalt experience. Not only the child, but also the adult experiences wholeness through the reading of literature. This is so because literature which is significant is art, and every piece of authentic art possesses wholeness. The meaning of art, of literature, is present because of the wholeness of the work of art. Meaning is destroyed when wholeness is destroyed.

Beyond the representation of a work of art, a meaning awaits discovery. The reader who is open to receive, discovers meaning and from the meaning he receives insights. Insights happen through keeping the meaning intact, not through analysis. The wholeness of a gestalt experience is for anyone who comes to art, learning, and life, not with an analytical attitude, but with the openness of the person becoming whole.

In this discussion the reading of literature has been used as an example of an experience of wholeness, and the library-centered approach has been seen as particularly appropriate to that experience. The literature of the other various disciplines provides opportunity for the learner to become whole through them and through an independent study approach to them. However, an experience of wholeness may not always be possible from one book or one art piece. The learner may need to read extensively in some disciplines in order to be able to center, structure, and discover. What is important is that each learner experience gestalts in his own way. What is equally important is that each learner discovers his way through a library-centered approach to learning.

Chapter Ten
Writing:
A Personal Response

Writing, the process of communicating through the use of the printed word, is a method of learning as well as an expression of learning. As a method of learning it is particularly appropriate to the library-centered, independent study approach.

The library-centered approach to learning realizes learning as an increase of consciousness which happens within the learner as he responds to any form of communication. A form of communication may be any tool of learning, any symbol which the learner reads, and the meaning beyond the tool and the symbol. The learner learns only through his personal response. One of the most personal ways for him to respond is through the act of writing.

Writing is a personal response because it is based on the needs of the individual learner and involves his whole person. According to the library-centered approach, the learner writes what and when he needs to write, not on topics and at times determined by another. Because writing is a felt need which is fulfilled by the learner, it has personal meaning for him.

The child in the library-centered primary school is free to write or print whatever has meaning for him. He will write and will learn to write well so long as he is motivated, and he is motivated to write when his needs are met. The child in the primary school loves to write words and entire stories which relate to his own experiences. He loves to learn those words which arise from his awareness of life. When freed to reveal the breadth and depth of his knowledge and understandings, the child proves that his own personal vocabulary is ever so much richer than that imposed upon him through a word list, a reader, or a text.

Through writing in a library-centered primary school, the child is enabled to match his individual learning needs with the entire range of the generic book provided in the library. The child's inspiration for writing comes from an interdisciplinary array of resources. The broad range of experiences provided by the library meet the varying needs of the individual learner as textbooks and classrooms never can.

As he writes, the child grows in knowledge and understanding of himself. He enjoys the sense of awakening which comes from writing. Through writing the learner becomes aware of what and how he thinks. As the learner reads his own writing, he comes to understand his ideas. As he concentrates on the printed word before him, he assimilates the meaning beyond it and becomes further integrated with it and within himself, since he is responsible for its being.

Through the act of writing, the learner not only comes to greater understanding of his ideas, but he also becomes more aware of his potential. He becomes aware of his capabilities and his limitations. As he reads, listens, and is receptive to the symbols and meanings of his life, he becomes increasingly aware of the impact which these have upon him, of the powers which permeate the world around him, and of the yet-to-be-tried potential of his human spirit.

Writing, a personal response to a form of communication, is not only based on individual learner needs, but also involves the whole person. The whole person of the writer: thoughts, feelings, and intuitions, are brought to bear upon the process of writing. Even as a child copies his favorite words on a piece of paper, he uses all of his powers. As he writes "football," he involves hand, arm, fingers, nerves, brain, eyes; and he thinks, feels, imagines, and remembers "football". In contrast, the child who is required to learn words from a list prescribed by another, may be using merely rote memory. However, the library-centered approach to learning, which is learner-centered, respects the needs and powers of the whole person.

Through his writing, inspired by the generic book, the child grows in knowledge of his world. As he writes, he learns. As he concentrates upon the symbols he uses and upon the meanings beyond them, he becomes increasingly conscious of the real world which he shares. Writing is for the child learner, as for every learner, a method of learning.

In addition to its being a method of learning, writing is also an expression of learning. As such it is a personal and integrating experience which promotes wholeness. As has been indicated, writing is personal because it is based on individual needs and because it involves the whole person in the process. Because it involves the whole person, writing is also an integrating experience. The writer brings all of his powers to bear on the process. The learner who writes in accord with his needs is not distracted. His thoughts, interests, and feelings are not separately vying for attention. Rather, he concentrates himself wholly upon the realization of his need. He experiences integration and wholeness as he is conscious of and realizes the here and now.

Writing is an expression of the wholeness which the learner enjoys. He expresses this wholeness in various ways. One way of communicating himself is through writing which reveals to himself his innermost thoughts, feelings, insights, and dreams.

The learner may have a special need to express himself through writing which is not intended to be read by another. He may need to write for the sake of growth in self-knowledge. By keeping a dairy, a daily log of his activities, or by recording his thoughts and feelings, and through reflection on this written expression, the learner experiences awareness of the growth process within himself. Such a written expression of his wholeness at any one time proves to the learner that he is in the process of growth. Even the primary school child sees evidence of learning and changing happening within himself.

Since a library-centered approach gives the learner opportunity to realize learning as a process, and since the process of learning can be expressed through the learner's written communication, the learner knows and understands this process as it happens within him, and through this experience, the learner comes to fuller realization of his identity.

The learner expresses this identity in his relationships with others. As reflection on his writing indicates to the learner the changes happening within him, he becomes aware of the changing quality of his personal relationships. He sees these human relationships as a dynamic process with limitless possibilities for integration and unity among mankind.

The writer expresses wholeness not only through his personal relationships with others, but also when he communicates his ideas, feelings, and insights with them. The writer shares his written expression, and therefore himself, with anyone who would care to read and to understand the meaning beyond the printed letters. This sharing of oneself with others strengthens the bond of interdependence which unites all learners. The learner who writes offers to everyone who would read the opportunity to grow in consciousness.

The tools which the writer uses to express himself include his vocabulary and his manner of using it. The words which the writer selects and the way in which he uses them are a part of his expression of a meaning. The choice and use of words are, therefore, of great importance if the fullest meaning is to be understood. These tools are essential and integrating elements of the process of communication. As symbols of a meaning they authentically express that meaning.

The process of writing is a creative process. It is a process of bringing into being a work of art; it is an authentic expression of an experience. Such a process can only be the work of an artist, but to be an artist requires that one is free. The library-centered approach respects the inherent freedom of the learner. Not being rigidly confined by teacher's assignments, course requirements, or other restrictive elements, the learner is free to create.

In this approach the learner reads widely and wisely. This broad exposure to ideas and feelings over a wide range of disciplines enriches the learner. Given time to assimilate his reading so that the learner becomes integrated with meanings, he creates himself and thereby readies himself for extending creation outside of himself. Creating through writing is therefore a natural expression and outflow of a library-centered experience of learning. According to this approach to learning, all learners are artists.

The example of writing considered as a creative process has indicated some possibilities for humanizing education and for liberating the learner. Teachers, administrators, and school systems may not be content with turning out efficient and knowledgeable individuals. To do so is to seal untapped the greatest human potential. To do so is to produce individuals productive as the latest technology, but with vital human powers locked in. The meaning beyond the process of education is the release of creative energies. Only an approach to learning which respects the freedom of the learner and which provides for the creation of the whole person can rightly be called true education.

✥
Chapter Eleven
Learning Through Insight

Learning which humanizes the educational environment and which liberates the learner provides for the creation of the whole person. Such a person frees his creative energies through use of all of his powers in responding to learning tools. One of these human powers is that of insight. Through the learning process the learner grows in realization of this power.

All learning is essentially insight. In this context insight is distinguished from an intellectual pursuit or a search for truth. The learner pursues ideas. He involves his energies in his quest for knowledge and for understandings. But none of these activities are synonymous with insight. Insight is not sought; it is received. An insight is a realization of wholeness. It is an awareness of reality. It is a union with truth. Insight happens to the learner. Because of insight, the learner changes; he grows. An approach to learning which respects this process of change is one which provides opportunity for insight. This chapter will attempt to show that the library-centered approach to learning best provides for insight to happen.

Although an insight can occur at any time and in any place, the environment of the library and the approach to learning which is library-centered are particularly appropriate to insightful learning. The primary requirement for insightful learning is that one listen. The library environment is an environment conducive to listening, not because of enforced library silence, but because of the super-abundance of learning tools replete with meaning waiting to be heard. Situated within this environment, the learner becomes sensitive to the possibilities for learning which surround him.

The learner listens to meanings. In his own individual way and motivated by his needs, he approaches the generic book, reads, listens, assimilates, and receives an insightful message. For example, the child in the library-centered primary school, motivated by his interest in dinosaurs, reaches for a picture book on this subject. He reads the pictures in the book, concentrates on what he reads, listens to what it tells him about dinosaurs, assimilates the meaning of dinosaurs, and expands his world through this increased consciousness of it. Because he has the freedom, the readiness, and the time to learn in his unique way, the child has also the opportunity for insight.

The library-centered approach to learning provides opportunity also for insight into solutions of problems. A part of life is learning how to approach and resolve problems. The ability to do this requires a self-concept secure in making decisions. The decision-making ability and the strength to assume responsibility for a decision are a part of the personal growth process. Therefore, the learner needs experience and opportunities for this process to evolve.

The library-centered approach to learning offers possibilities for growth in decision-making and in responsibility for these decisions. It also offers the learner opportunity to grow in consciousness of his insight and in his ability to resolve situations through insights received. This approach to learning offers the learner the experiences needed to form an attitude of reliance on insight, since this potential is acknowledged as contributing to the realization of the whole person.

The learner in the library-centered environment grows in decision-making ability as he assumes responsibility for his education. Through the library-centered approach he learns to know himself, his abilities and his limitations. He sets his goals and determines the means to them. He decides what he will read, and because of his internal motivation, he listens to the message, whether from printed page, film, or any other form of the generic book. He assimilates what he reads and makes it part of himself. The independent study aspect of library-centered learning encourages the learner to listen well to the possibilities from the learning tools which surround him, since through independent study the learner realizes himself in the process of creation. Throughout this process the learner listens for and receives insight.

The learner in the library listens not only for meanings and possible resolutions for practical problems, but he also listens to the aesthetic quality found in art and in all of life. The library-centered approach to learning is not limited to mind-training or exclusively intellectual matters. Rather, it respects the whole nature of the learner and provides for the creation of the whole person, affective as well as cognitive powers.

The learner listens therefore to his feelings and to whatever in his environment delights his sensibilities and assists in the creation of his affections. The learner listens, for example, to a sculptured art piece. He reads the symbolism of it, hears the message beyond the wood or marble, assimilates the meaning, and becomes united with it. He enjoys this kind of experience as one which is in accord with the requirements of his nature. He is not assigned to experience, to see, to listen. He cannot be assigned to receive an insight. Rather, the learner discovers this need within himself and learns to fulfill it.

The opportunities to listen to meanings, to listen for resolutions to problems, and to listen to art, are provided by a library-centered approach to learning. The library provides these opportunities since it provides opportunities for the learner to be personally involved with his education, and listening is a most meaningful way of personal involvement.

Although listening is a requisite for insightful learning, the learner cannot pursue insight. However, he can place himself in a learning situation and environment appropriate for insight to happen. Such an environment is one which not only encourages listening but is also a place characterized by tranquility. The learner cannot listen when he is agitated; he cannot concentrate when he is restless; and he cannot become whole without being single-minded in pursuit for the unity of truth. Therefore, the learner who would experience insight, first experiences that order required for peace.

Insightful learning also requires periods of reflection. The learner considers, ponders deeply, and thinks back upon his learning experiences. Through reflection upon these experiences the learner centers himself within the context of his whole life. He becomes aware of the structures which encompass his life and which are part of his world by the fact of his human nature. Through reflection the learner becomes aware of patterns in his life and of the evolving nature of his existence. Through reflection he can even enjoy a vision of the wholeness of his life. He can, in effect, experience a gestalt.

The child learner as well as the adult needs periods of reflection. He needs these according to his nature, not according to the wishes or assignments of another. The library-centered approach to learning provides opportunities for reflection because it respects time.

Just as insightful learning requires reflection, so too reflection requires time. Although an insight may be so quick as to be time-less, the learning situation in which an insight occurs is marked by a respect for time. The learner needs time. He needs time to think and time to put his life in perspective. The growth process cannot be hurried; nature demands time for growth. The library-centered and independent study approach to learning respects this demand of nature. That is why each learner enjoys whatever time he needs to center, structure, discover, listen, reflect, and integrate.

Although the requirements for insightful learning are applicable to all learners, the forms of insight are as unique as the learners who experience them. The child learner may experience insight into the relationships between the letters f-o-o-t-b-a-l-l and the picture of the object. The learner experiences insight into the relationship between the call number on a card catalog card and the location of the book on the shelf. Another learner experiences insight as he ponders the possibilities of creating a mosaic to express an idea. Still another learner experiences insight into the understanding of human suffering as he ponders the meaning of a painting.

The child learner enjoys the natural, simple openness appropriate to his age and therefore experiences insights readily and in accord with his nature. His expression of an insight may be simply, "Oh, I get it." The adult learner has the advantage of having experienced insights continually as a part of his learning and is therefore ready to further this aspect of his growth potential. Whether child or adult, all receive insights in the process of learning. Insights are possible in unique ways for all who would read, listen, reflect, and be patient.

The role of the facilitator in a learning environment which respects insight in the process of learning is that of encouraging the learner to discover his ways of receiving insights. The facilitator encourages the student to learn tranquility, to take time to listen and to reflect, and to be open to the life of the spirit which permeates his world.

Chapter Twelve
The Transcendental Dimension of the Learner

Previous chapters have indicated that in the process of becoming whole, the learner grows in consciousness and that he does this through the use of all of his powers. In addition to possessing powers of intellect and of his senses, the learner has also been described as having the capacity to receive insights. In this chapter a further dimension of the wholeness of the learner is considered through discussion of his transcendental nature.

The transcendental dimension of the learner includes his capacity for knowing, understanding, believing, and choosing through means other than sensible experience, intellectual pursuit, or insight. Rather, because of the transcendental dimension of his nature, the learner grows in consciousness and becomes whole also through the impact of the sum of these realities. The learner is not influenced by sensible or intellectual experiences considered as single, separate powers. Rather, he receives experiences as a whole, and is affected by the sum total of these experiences.

For example, the presence of a facilitator who is whole has an impact upon the learner not merely because of the overt behavior of the facilitator, but because of his spirit which animates him. This spirit cannot be dissected. The person of the facilitator is one, and it is as one whole being that he makes an impact, not because of any singular trait. Also, the facilitator who is whole influences the learner through honestly being himself, a whole person; therefore being honest in his relationship with the learner. In these cases, wholeness and honesty are recognized as transcendental realities, as being beyond the sum of the parts of the person.

The learner grows also because of the transcendental realities of the learning environment. He grows through these because the transcendental dimension of his nature responds to them. One such reality is that of trust. The trust present in the environment is known by the learner, although it cannot be defined. Neither can it be contained. Trust is present as a whole quality which is greater than the sum of all the ways in which it is present. It is as a whole reality that the trust has an impact upon the learner.

The transcendental dimension of the learner is evident in experiences of believing and choosing. As he realizes realities beyond the sensible, such as the meaning beyond the symbol, the learner deepens his awareness of realities beyond the sensible. He becomes increasingly conscious of the presence of transcendental realities within the world and of their impact upon him.

Because of the transcendental dimension of his nature, the learner makes choices not alone on the basis of sensible or intellectual knowledge, or even of insight, but on the basis of the wholeness he has become through evolution of all of his energies. This wholeness includes a reality which is transcendental. The wholeness of the learner is greater than the sum of his separate ways of knowing, understanding, believing, and choosing.

Through a library-centered approach to learning the learner experiences personal growth of his transcendental dimension, of his ability to know, understand, believe, and choose as an integrated whole person with every dimension of him influencing and affecting his whole being. Through this approach to learning the transcendental dimension is accepted as real for the learner, and the continual evolution of this dimension results in his further creation. In fact, the learner can become whole and fully created only when the transcendental dimension of his life is realized.

The learner in the library-centered environment selects a learning tool which has meaning for him. This simple action forms the basis for the evolution of the learner's transcendental dimension. It realizes the learner's need to know and to choose. This action realizes the learner's need to grow. As with other dimensions of the learner, such as his capacity for knowledge and insight, the transcendental dimension evolves. As with other kinds of growth, evolution of his transcendental nature is a continuous process and may not be interrupted. It is in harmony with other kinds of growth appropriate to the learner at various ages of his life. The library-centered approach to learning respects and builds on these basic needs for growth which are universal for all who would be whole.

As the learner grows in wholeness, he realizes personal growth and a further evolution of his transcendental nature. Through his transcendental nature the learner recognizes the wholeness of realities which affect his life. He knows too that he shares in the creative powers of these realities, and in sharing the creative power, the learner grows toward greater wholeness, greater unity within himself and with others.

The library-centered approach to learning provides the learner with the opportunity to recognize the wholeness of reality. The learner recognizes wholeness as he pursues ideas among the disciplines in a bibliographic way. He recognizes wholeness as he responds to problem-centered learning situations. He recognizes wholeness as he integrates his learning experiences within himself and with other learners.

Through this approach the learner realizes who he is and who another is. He realizes his relationships with others which include participation in the life of others and mutual responsibility for persons and the world. The learner realizes interdependence among others. Because of his transcendental dimension the learner has power to know meanings beyond the symbols which he reads in his relationships with others.

The learner grows in awareness of the interrelationships which unite the community of learners with each other and with their world. Because of his transcendental nature, he is other-directed. He is not locked within himself, but reaches out to others. He shares with others his ever-growing fulness of being. He is prompted to live not for himself alone, but for others.

An approach to learning which respects these realities is characterized by cooperation and a shared participation by the learners and facilitators in the ever broadening stream of creativity which results from shared learning. Each one teaches one to learn. In this approach to learning there is no place for competition, rivalries, jealousies, dean's lists, honor roles, or other destructive forces. Rather each one cooperates with the creative spirit of the other. Each learner brings other learners to life.

The transcendental dimension of the learner makes possible knowledge of the wholeness of life. Through experiencing himself in the process of creation, the learner comes to know the creative process which affects all of life. The whole of life, which is a process of creation, is seen as greater than all combined aspects of life.

The approach to learning which respects learning as a creative process respects thereby the transcendental nature of learning. Learning is realized as a process which reaches beyond the sensible and the intellectual, and even beyond insight. Learning is not limited to any one of the learner's powers or by the sum of the learner's energies. Rather, it is greater than the sum of all of his abilities. It is a creative process which cannot be contained. Learning is as mysterious and impenetrable as the mind of a child. However transcendent an activity, learning is not remote. It is as present as the learning tool which the learner selects; only its meanings cannot be fully fathomed.

As has been indicated throughout library-centered learning is an interdisciplinary approach accomplished through the generic book and the bibliographic way and offering the assistance of learning facilitators. The elements of this approach afford opportunity for the learner to grow in personal identity, respect for the other, interdependence with the other, shared participation in life, and the freedom to become whole and to share in the wholeness of the universe. Since the library-centered approach to learning provides for the creation of the learner through opportunities for increasing consciousness, it thereby builds on the transcendental nature of the learner. It does not set limits, but it opens even greater possibilities for exploration.

The learner selects his learning tool. He does so freely. The ramifications of this simple action cannot be encompassed with words. The realization of this simple, free action brings the learner to the fullest evolution of his being. Such free action is a share in the creative action of the cosmos. Surely, the greatest failure of anyone involved in the process of education is to inhibit this action, thereby destroying life, while the learner or facilitator who contributes to the creative process participates in a life-giving process. The learner selects a tool. This is the beginning of the penetration of meaning and mystery.

BIBLIOGRAPHY

Ashton-Warner, Sylvia. *Teacher.* New York: Simon and Schuster, 1963.

Berg, Paul C. "Classroom Practices in Teaching Reading" Paper presented at The International Reading Association Conference, May 6-9, 1970, Anaheim, California.

Blackie, John.*Transforming the Primary School.* New York: Schocken, 1974.

Branscomb, Harvie. *Teaching With Books.* Hamden, Conn.: Shoe String Press, 1964.

Brown, George I. "Affectivity, Classroom Climate, and Teaching" Washington, D.C.: Educational Monograph Series No. 6, May, 1971.

Bruner, Jerome S. "The Art of Discovery" *On Knowing: Essays for the Left Hand.* Cambridge, Mass.: Belknap Press of Harvard University Press, 1964. .81-96.

Bruner, Jerome S. "After John Dewey, What?" *On Knowing: Essays for the Left Hand.* Cambridge, Mass.: Belknap Press of Harvard University Press, 1964. 113—126.

Bruner, Jerome S. *Toward A Theory of Instruction.* Cambridge, Mass.: Belknap Press of Harvard University Press, 1967.

Carlyle, Thomas. *"The* Hero as Man of Letters" *On Heroes, Hero-Worship and the Heroic in History.* London: Oxford University Press, 1965. 154-195.

Castle, E.B. *The Teacher.* London: Oxford University Press, 1970.

Clayton, Howard and Robert T. Jordan. "Library-College"*The Encyclopedia of Education.* New York: Macmillan, 1971.

Combs, Arthur W., Chairman A.S.C.D. Year Book Committee: *Perceiving Behaving Becoming.* Washington, D.C.- National Education Association, 1962.

Curry, Robert L. and Gene D. Shepherd. "Learning in a Personalized Media Environment" *The Library-College Journal,* III (Spring, 1970), 28-32.

Dinkmeyer, Don. "The C-Group: Focus on Self as Instrument" *Phi Delta Kappan,* LII (June, 1971), 617-619.

Donelson, Kenneth L. "The New Literature" *Arizona English Bulletin,* XIII (October, 1970), 8-13.

Bibliography

Eble, Kenneth. *A Perfect Education.* New York: Macmillan, 1966.

Eysenck, H.J., ed. "Ganzheit: gestalt; structure" *Encyclopedia of Psychology.* New York: Herder and Herder, 1972. 4-8.

Fillmer, H. Thompson. "Personality Type and Achievement in Reading." Paper presented at Annual Meeting of International Reading Association, May 10-13, 1972, Detroit, Michigan.

Frost, Robert. "The Road Not Taken" *The Poems of Robert Frost.* New York: Modern Library, 1946.

Furst, Norma and Russell A. Hill. "Classroom Observation, Systematic" (The *Encyclopedia of Education.* New York: Macmillan, 1971. 168-183.

Gaylor, Robert. "The Philosophy of the Last Frontier" *The Library College Journal,* II (Summer, 1969), 35-40.

Getzels, J.W. and P.W. Jackson. "The Teacher's Personality and Characteristics" *Handbook of Research on Teaching.* Chicago: Rand McNally, 1963. 506-582.

Gibran, Kahlil. *The Prophet.* New York: Knopf, 1965.

Gingell, Lesley P. *The ABC's of the Open Classroom.* Homewood, Ill.: ETC, 1973.

Glasser, William. *Schools Without Failure.* New York: Harper & Row, 1969.

Goldenson, Robert M. "Gestalt Psychology" *The Encyclopedia of Human Behavior, Psychology, Psychiatry, and Mental Health.* New York: Doubleday, 1970. 505-509.

Graziano, Eugene Edward. *Language-Operational-Gestalt-Awareness A Radically Empirical and Pragmatical Phenomenology of the Processes and Systems of Library Experience.* Tempe, Arizona: The Association for Library Research Communications, 1975.

Green, Donald Ross. *Educational Psychology.* Englewood Cliffs, N.J.: Prentice-Hall, 1964.

Hilgard, Ernest R. *Theories of Learning. 2nd ed.* New York· Appleton-Century-Crofts, 1956.

Hillerich, Robert L. "Evaluation of Written Language" Paper presented at the Annual Meeting of the American Educational Research Association, March, 1970, Minneapolis, Minnesota.

Holt, John. *How Children Fail.* New York: Pitman, 1964.

Holt, John. *How Children Learn.* New York: Pitman, 1967.

Bibliography

Holt, John. *The Underachieving School.* New York: Pitman, 1969.

Holt, John. *What Do I Do Monday?* NNew York: Dutton, 1970.

Hostrop, Richard W. *Education Inside the Library-Media Center.* Hamden, Conn.: Shoe String Press. 1973.

Hostrop, Richard W. "Learning and the Library-College" *The Library-College Journal, IV* (Spring, 1971), 35-41.

Hoveland, Carl I. "Human Learning and Retention" *Handbook of Experimental Psychology. New York:* John Wiley, 1951. 613-689.

Husen, Torsten. *The Learning Society.* London, Methuen 1974.

James, Muriel and Dorothy Jongeward. *Born to Win: Transactional Analysis with Gestalt Experiences.* Reading, Mass.: Addison-Wessley, 1971.

Jennings, Frank G. *This is Reading.* New York: Dell, 1965.

Jerome, Judson. "Radical Premises in Collegiate Reform" *Annals of the American Academy of Political and Social Science. 404:* (November 1972), 194-206.

Johnson, B. Lamar. *Vitalizing A College Library.* Chicago: American Library Association, 1939.

Kersh, Bert Y. and Merl C. Wittrock. "Learning by Discovery: An Interpretation of Recent Research" *The Journal of Teacher Education,* XIII (December, 1962), 461-468.

Kohler, Wolfgang. Gestalt Psychology. New York: The New American Library, 1947.

Krishnamurti, Juddi. *Education and the Significance of Life.* New York: Harper & Row, 1953.

McClintock, Robert "Universal Voluntary Study" *The Center Magazine, VI:* no. 1 (January-February, 1973), 24-30.

Martin, Everett Dean. The *Meaning of a Liberal Education. New York:* Norton, 1926.

Melby, Ernest O. *The Teacher and Learning. New York:* The Center for Applied Research in Education, 1963.

Nichols, Shirley. "Pupil Motivation: A Rewarding Experience" *Maryland English Journal,* VIII (Spring, 1970), 36-41.

Pestalozzi, Heinrich. *The Education of Man: Aphorisms.* New York: Greenwood Press, 1951.

Bibliography

Postman, Neil and Charles Weingartner. *Teaching As A Subversive Activity*. New York: Delacorte Press, 1969.

Ray, Willis E. "Pupil Discovery vs. Direct Instruction" *Journal of Experimental Education*, XXIX (March, 1961), 271-280.

Renfield, Richard. *If Teachers Were Free*. Washington, D.C.: Acropolis, 1969.

Rogers, Carl R. "Bringing Together Ideas and Feelings in Learning" *Learning Today*, V (Spring, 1972), 32-43.

Rogers, Carl R. *Freedom to Learn*. Columbus, Ohio: Merrill, 1969.

Rosenthal, Robert. *Pygmalion in the Classroom*. New York: Holt, Rinehart, & Winston, 1968.

Rowland, Howard S. *No More School*. New York: Dutton, 1975.

Ryans, David G. Characteristics of Teachers: *Their Description, Comparison, and Appraisal; A Research Study*. Washington, D.C.: American Council on Education, 1960.

Ryans, David G. "Research on Teacher Behavior in the Context of the Teacher Characteristics Study" *Contemporary Research on Teacher Effectiveness. New York: H*olt, Rinehart & Winston, 1964. 67-101.

Schadt, Armin L. *A Counterfeit Reality: The Education of Post-Faustian Man*. North Quincy, Mass.: Christopher Publishing House, 1975.

Schwab, Joseph J. "Learning Community" *The Center Magazine*, VIII, no. 3 (May-June, 1975), 30-44.

Sheehan, Sister Helen. "Implementing the Library-College Idea" *The Library-College Journal, I* (Summer, 1968), 15-19.

Sheehan, Sister Helen. "The Library-College Idea: Trend of the Future?" *Library Trends*, XVIII (July, 1969), 93-102.

Shores, Louis: Robert Jordan; John Harvey, eds. *The Library-College*. Philadelphia: Drexel Press, 1966.

Shores, Louis. "The Library-College Idea" *Library Journal*, XIC (September 1, 1966), 3871-3875.

Shores, Louis. *Library-College USA*. Tallahassee, Florida: South Pass Press, 1970.

Shores, Louis. "The Medium School" *Phi Delta Kappan*, XLVIII (February, 1967), 285-288.

Bibliography

Shores, Louis. "The Medium Way" *The Library-College Journal, I* (Winter), 1968), 10-17.

Sillers, Dan J. "New Dimensions in Innovation" *The Library-College Journal,* IV (Winter, 1971), 10-11.

Sillers, Dan J. "Practical Aspects on the Library-College Idea" *Catholic Library World, XL* (November, 1968), 182-183.

Soar, Robert S. "Optimum Teacher-Pupil Interaction for Pupil Growth" *Educational Leadership, XXVI (*December, 1968 supplement), 275-280.

Soar, Robert S. "Research Findings from Systematic Observation" *Journal of Research and Development in Education, IV* (Fall, 1970), 116-122.

Soar, Robert S. "Teacher Behavior Related to Pupil Growth" *International Review of Education,* XVIII (1972), 508-528.

Spence, Kenneth W. "Theoretical Interpretations of Learning" *Handbook of Experimental Psychology. New York:* John Wiley, 1951. 690-729.

Tennyson, Alfred Tennyson, baron, "Ulysses" *The Poems and Plays of Alfred Lord Tennyson. New York:* Modern Library, 1938. 166-168.

Ternent, William A. "Planning for a Student Directed, Student Evaluated Learning Situation" Paper presented at the Convention of the International Communication Association, April, 1972, Atlanta, George.

Wertheimer, Max. *Productive Thinking. New York:* Harper & Brothers, 1959.

Whitman, Walt. "There was a child went forth" *Leaves of Grass.* New York: Modern Library, n.d. 288-289.

INDEX

Analysis. 90-91

Art. 20, 27, 91, 95, 97-98

Artist 15, 20, 51, 95

Attitudes, positive. 13-14, 58, 87

Awareness . 1, 3, 6-7, 35-36, 94, 101

Bibliographic approach to learning
. 33-34

Bibliographically expert faculty
. . . . 38-41, 52, 70, 72

Card catalog. 45-47, 61, 63, 65

Carlyle, Thomas 78, 83

Centering. 47, 81, 88

Choice. . . 10, 19, 29, 36, 56-57, 101

Communication 2, 28, 40

Community 40, 84
. . . . of learners. . . . 28, 102

Consciousness. . .1, 5, 35, 79, 82, 97

Convictions 29-30

Cooperation. 28, 102

Creative ability 7

Creative energies 2, 5, 49
. . . . .77, 85, 95

Curriculum. 34, 74

DESIRERATA 84

Decision-making ability 27, 36
. . . . 56-57, 97

Disciplines. 77-78

Discovery approach to learning
. 24-25

Education 16-17, 23, 85
goal of. 3
purpose of 2

EDUCATION INSIDE THE
LIBRARY-MEDIA CENTER. . . .22

Evolution. 78, 80, 101, 103

Failure 8, 50, 73-74, 103

Fear 3, 52
of failure 27, 58

Freedom 2-4, 16-17, 78, 89

Frost, Robert 10

Fully-functioning person. 8-9
. . . . 13-14, 83

Generalist 40

Generic book 32-33, 42, 64

Gestalt 82, 89-91, 98

Gibran, Kahlil. 12

Growth 1, 15, 17, 22, 74, 101

Holt, John 5, 7

Hostrop, Richard W. 22

Humility 6, 18

Ideals 16

Identity. 8, 19, 28, 78, 84, 94

Independence. 3, 8-9

Independent study. 35-41
. . . . 43-44, 48-49

Indirect teaching. 25

Individuation 8

Inner-relatedness. 19, 81

Insight. 79, 82-84, 88, 91
. 96-99

Integration. . . 34, 80, 83, 88-89, 94

Integrity 7, 15, 30

Interaction. 28, 60, 72, 77

Interpendence. 9, 60, 94, 102

Interdisciplinary learning 34
. 58-59

Learning, life-long 3, 40

Learning tools. 48, 52, 61, 103

Lesson plan 53-54, 56

Listening 5-7, 28, 87, 96-98

Love. 15-17

Martin, Everett Dean 4-5

Maturity 1, 22, 27

Meaning. 23-24, 57, 80-82, 85
. . . . .87-91, 96, 101

Motivation. 17, 22, 58, 61

Openness. . . .3-7, 17, 36, 41, 87, 91

Organic learning 48

Pacing. 26

Pattern 9, 82, 98

Periodical index 46-47, 70-71

Pestalozzi, Heinrich 2, 17, 85

Power
of creation. 3, 7
of discovery 24
of senses 26, 35
of insight. 96
to choose. 27

Powers, human 100

PROPHET, THE.12

PYGMALION. 18

PYGMALION
IN THE CLASSROOM 18

Reading. 35-36, 50, 63, 72-73
. . . . 77-78, 86-91

Reflection 98

Relationships 4, 13, 28, 47, 78
. . . . .78-84, 94, 102

Respect. 16, 29

Response. 1-2, 5, 9-10, 92-93

Rogers, Carl 3

Rosenthal, Robert 18

Security 3, 27, 58

Seeking behavior 26

Self-concept 8, 13-14, 27

Self-creation, 3, 17, 20, 82-84

Self-expression 7-8, 26, 28

Self-knowledge 6-7, 27, 35,
. . . . 83, 93-94

Self-selection 26

Shaw, George Bernard 18

Shores, Louis 32

Socrates 14-15

Specialist 40
SEE ALSO Bibliographically
expert faculty

Spirit, of facilitator 87, 100

Spirit, of learning 4

Structure 9-10, 47, 55, 73
. . . . .76, 82, 88

Structural requirements 23, 55
. . . . .73, 79, 88-89

Structuring 81

Success 26, 40, 49, 52

Symbols 86-90, 93-95

Symbols, classification 46, 63

Tennyson, Alfred Lord 3-4

Time 98-99

Tools of learning
. . . . SEE Learning Tools

Trust 29, 52, 100-101
of self 8, 27, 49

Truth 7, 15, 18-19, 83

Truth-seeking 4-5

ULYSSES 3-4

Uniqueness 28, 49, 60, 85

Values 19-20, 29, 36-37

Whitman, Walt 9

Wholeness . . . 8-9, 17, 47, 53, 76-84
. . . . 91, 100-103

Wisdom 19

Writing 92-95